THE GOLFER'S COOKBOOK

Recipes Collected at Pebble Beach

THE GOLFER'S COOKBOOK

Maureen Chodosh & Maggie Weiss

Hurtig Publishers
Edmonton

Hurtig Publishers Ltd.
10560–105 Street
Edmonton, Alberta
Canada T5H 2W7

Canadian Cataloguing in Publication Data

Chodosh, Maureen.
    The golfer's cookbook

Includes index.
ISBN 0-88830-274-6

1. Cookery, American - California. 2. Golf
courses - California. I. Weiss, Maggie J.
II. Title.
TX715.C496 1984   641.5   C84-091543-8

Jacket illustration: 18th green at Pebble Beach golf links, Pebble Beach, California

Photography Credits
Photography: Al Weber, Carmel, California
Food Styling: Tom King, San Aptosuz, California
Design: Two's Co./Cookbooks, Pebble Beach, California
Table Settings: Allen & Company, Carmel, California
Flower Arrangements: Flowers Ltd., Pebble Beach, California

Production Credits
Editor: Maralyn Horsdal, Fulford Harbour, British Columbia
Designer: David Shaw & Associates Ltd., Toronto, Ontario
Composition: Attic Typesetting Inc., Toronto, Ontario
Manufacturer: D.W. Friesen & Sons, Altona, Manitoba

Printed and bound in Canada

Contents

With much love we dedicate this book to our families:

Norman, Leonard, David and Fran Chodosh, and
Cynthia, Mark, and Lisa Pepper

who have provided their encouragement,
support and enthusiasm.

Foreword

Some golfers may feel they're in the rough or a sand trap when they get in the kitchen. Others can get in the swing and turn out some classic dishes. As for me, when it comes to cooking I'm a 'hacker'. I've been known to burn water. One recipe said to take one egg and beat it, so I left the house for three days. Another one told me to scald the milk and I didn't know how much hot water to use. I was really upset when one recipe told me to baste a chicken and I can't even thread a needle.

But seriously, you'll find some great recipes in the Golfers' Cookbook. One must eat well to keep up to par. My diet must include greens—on the course and on the table. Now, if you're lucky and don't have to watch your waistline, Maggie Weiss has a great recipe for Banana Balls. However, whatever your handicap, I know you'll find recipes to suit you to a tee.

Bob Hope

October, 1984

Introduction

"How did you ever think of that idea?" is the question we are most frequently asked in regard to this book. Maureen and her husband were at a cocktail party with fellow golfers and all were discussing their game. As the evening progressed, the men carried on with golf stories and the women moved on to another favorite subject—cooking. Someone quipped, "Why not a cookbook compiling recipes from our favorite golfers?"

The idea stuck and was further developed by Maureen and Maggie during early morning walks along the ocean in Carmel, with Pebble Beach Golf Links across the bay. "Why not collect recipes from leading golf professionals and celebrities interested in golf?" "Why not photograph the spectacular golf courses on the Monterey Peninsula and combine the pictures with recipes collected from golfers?" "Why not involve the Crosby Youth Fund, which sponsors the Crosby Pro-Am Golf Tournament, better known as 'The Crosby Clambake' at Pebble Beach each year?"

"The Crosby" was started by Bing Crosby in 1937 at Rancho Santa Fe, near San Diego, as a "gathering of friends" from the golfing world, both professional and amateur. The tournament was played at Rancho Santa Fe for the first six years, with a starting purse of $2,500 and a top of $5,000, before it was discontinued during the war years.

It was moved to Pebble Beach in 1947. The first purse, after the tournament came to the Monterey Peninsula, was $10,000. And the tournament, at Bing's suggestion, was played over three courses—Pebble Beach, Cypress Point and the Monterey Peninsula Country Club—the first official tournament in America to be played over more than one course at the same time. Later, when Spyglass Hill course was opened in 1967, it was substituted for the Country Club as the third course.

In 1968, the tournament went "big time", expanding from three days to four for 72 holes; the purse was hiked from $15,000 to $50,000 and play was televised coast to coast for the first time. From then on, the tournament, like

1

Topsy, just "growed", until today, it has a purse of $440,000 and TV ratings that top those of all other golf tournaments year after year.

All proceeds from the tournament have always gone to the Bing Crosby Youth Fund, a private charitable foundation. The board of trustees distributes these funds to selected youth-oriented organizations in the Monterey Bay area. A portion of the proceeds from the sale of this book will be donated to the Crosby Youth Fund. We are proud to be associated with this charitable organization.

The interest and response of the people we approached were overwhelming. All were enthusiastic, giving, and sincerely interested in the project. We have met and spoken with fascinating people who encouraged us and offered us their expertise.

At one point in the process of gathering our collection, we were very "long" on chicken, chili and chocolate. Thanks to Maralyn Horsdal, our editor, we now have a balanced book, with over 300 recipes. The golfers' recipes decidedly follow the trend of California cuisine. And, in supplementing them with recipes from our own files and from friends, we very definitely kept this in mind. Since most of our readers want to spend more time outdoors, these recipes are easy, fast, and fun to make. From the recipe "Two Cans and One Box!" to the more complex "Dilled Caviar Puffs", there is something for everyone. Special low-fat, calorie-wise recipes appear at the end of the sections; see "Chocolate Soufflé Viennese", for instance, at the end of "Desserts".

Eagerness and dedication were the main ingredients for this venture. Since two heads are definitely better than one, we always bounced ideas off one another until the desired effect was achieved. We both loved each and every stage of this book. Every detail was discussed: from the layout of the recipes to the size of typeface used, to collecting the perfect props for the food photographs. Trying out the recipes on family and friends was a delight for all. We hope you find this book comprehensive, innovative and functional. We want it to be a welcome addition to your cookbook library.

Maureen Chodosh
Maggie Weiss

History of Pebble Beach

Located 120 miles south of San Francisco, this dramatic setting features the Pebble Beach Golf Links, overlooking Carmel Bay and Stillwater Cove, with commanding views of Point Lobos and the Santa Lucia Mountains: a vision of green and golden hills, safe from the crashing ocean tides and steep surrounding cliffs.

In 1908, Samuel F.B. Morse, a young man from Massachusetts, came to work for the Pacific Improvement Company, a subsidiary of Southern Pacific Railway. His foresight and love for this peninsula were the force behind Del Monte Properties. He presided over the company until his death in 1969. With the aid of Herbert Fleischacker and other influential San Francisco friends, he purchased land which now includes the Del Monte Forest with its six golf courses, the Del Monte Lodge and shops, the famed Seventeen-Mile Drive, many homes, and tons of white sand, as well as a handle on the economy of the towns of Monterey, Carmel-by-the-Sea and Pacific Grove.

The game of golf was certainly known in the west before the coming of Mr. Morse. For nearly two decades, aficionados had been playing Monterey Del Monte Course, in the forest in the west which then was part of the vast holdings of William H. Crocker. In the early 1900s, the Del Monte Course, an adjunct of the flamboyant Del Monte Hotel (now the Naval Postgraduate School) was the site of an annual golf tournament which became the California State Amateur Championship. Morse commissioned a two-time State Amateur champion, Jack Neville, to lay out Pebble Beach Golf Links. Neville called in two of his close golfing friends, Douglas Grant and H. Chandler Egan, to help him with the bunkering and undulations. Using a rough figure-eight outline, he made the most of the existing terrain. From that day to the present, the layout has not been changed, except for some small refinements. The course was opened for play in 1919, coincidental with the opening of the present Del Monte Lodge. (The original lodge was destroyed by fire in 1917.) Pebble Beach quickly became the mecca of western golf, a showplace for celebrities and a playground for socialites, millionaires and royalty.

In 1925, the Dunes Course of the Monterey Peninsula Country Club was molded into the forest, followed by the completion of Cypress Point Golf Course. Cypress, designed by Alistair MacKenzie and completed in 1928 on top of a prehistoric Indian graveyard, is said to be like a gorgeous woman: breathtakingly beautiful and terribly demanding. The picturesque 16th hole is probably the most photographed of all golf holes. Cypress Point and Pebble Beach so impress visitors that they have been called "the two finest courses in the world".

In March 1967, Spyglass Hill was added to this golfers' paradise. An exacting and exciting course, it ended the controversy between Pebble and Cypress. Some say it's more beautiful, and most say it is tougher, than either. The Peter Hay Course, a pitch-and-putt public layout adjacent to Pebble Beach, named for the late, well-known professional at both Del Monte and Pebble, was added to complement this center of sporting and social activities on the Monterey Peninsula.

Two more golf courses are planned for Pebble Beach. One will be the Northern California Golf Association's home course, to be constructed near the center of the forest, and the other will be a resort hotel and golf course at Spanish Bay, adjacent to Pacific Grove. The Del Monte Company will develop and operate the latter, in this area scarred by years of sand-mining.

Pebble Beach is known as "The Golf Capital of the World". Visitors return home, awed by the magnificence of the setting, the whimsy of the weather and the grandeur of the architecture. Ask a dozen leading professionals to name their top ten courses and Pebble will appear on every list. Pebble Beach, of those in the area, is unquestionably the best known, nationally and internationally. Its association with the Bing Crosby National Invitational Tournament, which has been played there since 1947, has led to its worldwide fame.

Acknowledgements

We would like to thank all of our friends who have encouraged, listened, and shared their recipes with us: Vada Beard, Shannon Baker, Paul Boczkowski, Carol Buchert, Carmel Wet Fish Market, David Chodosh, Marilyn Cole, Anne Foudy, Friedman's Microwave Ovens, Theodora H. Jensen, Alana Keifer, Pat Mewhinney, Linda Christiansen Morrison, Chris Petrow, Dukie Petrow, Ina E. Prosser, Barbara Schlesinger, Diane Watson, and Judy Walser.

To Lillian Eccher, Shirley Mattraw, and Sherri Waldman , thank you for your imagination and support. Thank you also to our friends whose recipes wound up on the cutting-room floor.

A special thank you to Kathryn Crosby and Carmel Martin, Jr., who helped us from day one.

Thank you to the PGA, the LPGA, Wyn Hope, and Ted Durein, who have contributed to the success of this book. We gratefully acknowledge our photographers, Batista Moon Studio, John Howard, and Al Weber, who brought the food and the terrain to life. A special thank you to our food stylists, Megan Lenders and Tom King.

OOOOOOOOOOOOOOOOOOOOO

Appetizers

OOOOOOOOOOOOOOOOOOOOO

Hot Artichoke Cheese Dip
Bruce Fleisher

At the tender age of 19, Bruce won the 1968 United States
Amateur Championship—the first of many victories. When
they're at home in Miami, Florida, Bruce and his wife,
Wendy, like entertaining, often beginning the evening
with this easy and elegant dish.

Yield: 2 cups

1 6-ounce can artichoke hearts, packed in water
1 cup mayonnaise
1 cup grated Parmesan cheese

Preheat oven to 350 degrees.
1. Chop artichoke hearts into very fine pieces.
2. Add mayonnaise and cheese; mix together thoroughly.
3. Bake in casserole dish for 20-30 minutes at 350 degrees
   or until brown and bubbly.
4. Serve with crackers.

Bacon Sticks   Microwave

Something different to serve with cocktails! Can be assembled in advance and stay crisp several hours after microwaving.

Yield: 10 sticks

10 thin bread sticks, any flavor
5 slices bacon, halved lengthwise
½ cup grated Parmesan cheese

1. Dredge one side of bacon strip in cheese; roll it against bread stick diagonally, cheese side in.
2. Place sticks on baking sheet, dish or paper plate lined with paper towels.
3. Microwave on High 4½ to 6 minutes. Roll again in cheese.

Dilly Beans

These beans have a real kick to them! (See photograph)

Yield: About 1 gallon

4 pounds green beans, fresh
2 quarts water
1 tablespoon coarse salt (kosher)
2 teaspoons mustard seed
¼ cup dill weed
4 cloves garlic

1. Wash beans, cut off ends and leave whole. Boil water, add salt. Add beans.
2. Boil beans, uncovered, 5 minutes or until tender crisp. Drain and cool.
3. In a large jar, put the mustard seed, dill weed, and garlic. Add beans to the jar.
4. Make brine.

Brine

2 cups water
2 cups white vinegar
²/₃ cup sugar
2 tablespoons coarse salt (kosher)
1 teaspoon crushed, dried, hot chili pepper
1 teaspoon dill seed

5. Bring water, vinegar, sugar, salt, chili pepper and dill seed to a boil.
6. Pour over the beans; cool and refrigerate.
7. Let age several weeks, if possible. Serve as finger food.

Brie with Glazed Almonds

Your guests will ask for this recipe!! (See photograph)

Yield: 16-20 servings

1 34-ounce wheel of Brie, at room temperature
2 tablespoons powdered sugar*
½ cup sliced almonds*
10 seedless red grapes, halved
thin slices of French bread or brioche

1. Scrape rind from top of cheese.
2. Sift 1 tablespoon powdered sugar evenly over surface. Arrange sliced almonds over top, pressing firmly into place.
3. Preheat broiler. Line baking sheet with foil. Place cheese on foil. Sift remaining 1 tablespoon powdered sugar over cheese. Broil 6-8 inches from heat, turning cheese as necessary, until top is evenly browned. Watch carefully as sugar caramelizes quickly.
4. Using foil as aid, transfer cheese to serving platter. Cut away as much foil as possible and garnish with grapes.

> *You may substitute brown sugar and pecans for the powdered sugar and almonds. Omit grapes.
> Can be prepared a day in advance before broiling. Use container to store in refrigerator and bring to room temperature before broiling.

Caviar Pie

Serve in small wedges with small rounds of thinly-sliced rye bread.

Yield: 1 9-inch pie

1 pound cream cheese, softened
1 egg yolk
¼ teaspoon dried, crumbled basil
¼ teaspoon garlic salt
5 ounces caviar
4 scallions, finely chopped
2 hard-cooked eggs, grated

1. Line mold (a 9-inch pie plate works well) with plastic wrap.
2. Beat softened cream cheese with egg yolk. Add basil and garlic salt; beat well.
3. Fill mold with mixture and refrigerate 20-30 minutes or until firm.
4. Unmold and garnish with caviar, scallions and eggs.

 Boiled eggs should never be boiled, just simmered. There is no such thing as hard-boiled eggs...they're hard-cooked eggs!

Dilled Caviar Puffs

A very professional appetizer. This will dress up your next cocktail party. (See photograph)

Yield: About 48 servings

Puffs

6 tablespoons unsalted butter, cut into bits
1 teaspoon salt
⅛ teaspoon white pepper
1 cup water
1 cup all-purpose flour, sifted
4 eggs

Filling

½ pound cream cheese, softened
2 tablespoons mayonnaise
1 tablespoon sour cream
2 tablespoons dill (fresh, if possible)
1 tablespoon fresh lemon juice
1 large, hard-cooked egg, sliced
¼ teaspoon Worcestershire sauce
white pepper and salt to taste
2 tablespoons salmon caviar
2 tablespoons black caviar
2 tablespoons golden caviar (optional)

Preheat oven to 425 degrees.

1. To make the puffs, combine in a heavy saucepan the butter, salt, and white pepper with water, and bring to a boil, stirring occasionally.
2. Remove the pan from the heat and stir in the flour all at once.
3. Cook the mixture over low heat, beating, for 2 minutes. Remove the pan from the heat; add the eggs, 1 at a time, beating well after each addition.
4. Transfer the dough to a pastry bag fitted with a ½-inch plain tip, pile 1-inch mounds of it 2 inches apart on lightly buttered baking sheets and bake them for 20 minutes, or until they are puffed and golden.
5. Let the puffs cool on racks, slice off the tops, reserving them, and discard any uncooked dough inside the puff.

Filling

6. In a food processor, fitted with a steel blade, or in a blender, blend the cream cheese, mayonnaise, sour cream, dill, lemon juice, egg, Worcestershire sauce, white pepper and salt until mixture is smooth.
7. Chill the filling, covered, for 1 hour or until it is firm.
8. With a small spoon, stuff the puffs with the filling.
9. Decorate with the different caviars. Replace the reserved tops.

Cheese Ball   Tom Kite

Tom is a born-and-bred Texan and one of the favorites on the tour. With many wins to his credit, he is a Million Dollar Winner. No need to worry about a "slice" when you approach this hors d'oeuvre. The combination of cheese, onions and chipped beef gives it an unusual taste.

Yield: 1 cheese ball

1 8-ounce package cream cheese, softened
1-2 green onions, finely chopped
1 teaspoon Accent
1 teaspoon Worcestershire sauce
1 package chipped or corned beef

1. Combine cheese with onions, Accent and Worcestershire sauce.
2. Form a ball and roll in chipped beef.
3. Serve with crackers or bread rounds.

Mexican Cheese Balls

Cheese and nuts on a roll.

Yield: 24 balls

2 8-ounce packages cream cheese, softened
2 tablespoons minced green pepper
2 tablespoons chopped pimento
1 ½ tablespoons finely minced onion
salt to taste
cream
1 cup pine nuts or chopped walnuts

1. Add green pepper, pimento, onion and salt to cream cheese, with enough cream to soften mixture.
2. Form into bite-sized balls and roll in nuts; chill.

Cheese and Bacon Spread
Michael Brannan

Mike Brannan now calls Arizona home. Born in Salinas, California, Mike turned professional in 1978. This is his easy and tasty spread to serve with drinks.

Yield: 2 cups

3 8-ounce packages cream cheese, softened
1 bunch green onions, chopped
1 pound bacon, fried and crumbled
3 ounces Parmesan cheese, shredded

Preheat oven to 300 degrees.
Mix all ingredients together. Heat in oven at 300 degrees for 20 minutes. Serve with small rounds of thinly sliced rye bread.

1-2-3 in a Crock

You're always ready with a delicious appetizer. This will keep for about three months in the refrigerator.

Yield: 2 cups

1 pound sharp Cheddar cheese, grated
1/2 pound blue cheese, crumbled
2 3-ounce packages cream cheese, softened
1/2 cup white wine
1/4 cup dry sherry
1 teaspoon Worcestershire sauce
2 tablespoons grated raw onion
5 dashes liquid red pepper sauce
1 clove garlic, minced

Combine all ingredients and mix thoroughly; chill. Serve as a spread with rye bread or crackers.

Muddled Chestnuts

Serve these with lots of napkins!

Yield: 6-8 servings

1 pound fresh chestnuts
½ cup port wine
¼ cup sugar

Preheat oven to 400 degrees.
1. With a sharp, pointed knife, cut a slit about ½-inch long through shell into meat of each chestnut. Discard any chestnuts that are moldy.
2. Arrange nuts in a single layer on a baking sheet.
3. Bake in a 400-degree oven for 40 minutes.
4. Mix port and sugar in a deep bowl. Remove chestnuts from oven.
5. Wearing oven mitts, squeeze each nut to pop the shell open so it can absorb the port, and drop into port-sugar mixture, stirring with each addition.
6. Let stand, stirring occasionally, until cool enough to touch.

Chili Rellenos Hors d'oeuvres

So easy and so good.

Yield: 8 servings

12 ounces Monterey Jack cheese
6 ounces medium or sharp Cheddar cheese
1 4-ounce can green chilies, mild or hot
2 eggs
2 tablespoons light cream or evaporated milk
1½ teaspoons flour

Preheat oven to 375 degrees.
1. Grate all the cheese and mix together.
2. Remove seeds from the chilies and cut them into thin strips.

3. Grease a 9 × 9-inch pan and alternate layers of cheese and chili strips, beginning and ending with a cheese layer.
4. Beat the eggs, cream and flour together and pour mixture over layered ingredients.
5. Bake at 375 degrees for 40 minutes. Cut into small squares and serve warm.

Chili Relleno Dip   Charles Coody

Lynette Coody claims this is "Charlie's favorite chip and dip!" Charles, the 1971 Masters winner, claims this will probably be your favorite dip, too!

Yield: 1½ cups

1 3½-ounce can chopped black olives
1 4-ounce can chopped green chilies
2 tomatoes, chopped
4 green onions, tops and all, chopped
3 tablespoons salad oil
1½ tablespoons vinegar
1 teaspoon salt
1 teaspoon garlic salt
1 teaspoon pepper

Mix all ingredients together.
Serve with any kind of chips.

Green Chili Cheese Dip Jack Doss

A typical California chili dip to accompany a drink when you're relaxing and rehashing your favorite round of golf. Jack hopes to see you at Pasatiempo Golf Club in Santa Cruz, California, where he is the professional.

Yield: About 3 cups

1 16-ounce box Velveeta cheese
4 4-ounce cans diced green chilies
1 medium tomato, finely chopped

1. Melt together the cheese and green chilies.
2. Before serving, add the finely chopped tomato, squeezed dry. Put in a chafing dish, surrounded by tortilla chips.

Banana Balls

Guaranteed...straight down the middle!!

Yield: 1 dozen

12 bacon slices, cut in half
6 bananas, slightly underripe
½ cup brown sugar
1 tablespoon curry powder

Preheat oven to 350 degrees.
1. Blanch bacon in boiling water approximately 10 minutes. Drain and dry thoroughly.
2. Slice bananas into 1½-inch chunks and wrap in bacon slices, securing with a toothpick.
3. Combine brown sugar and curry powder. Roll bacon-banana balls in brown sugar and curry powder mixture.
4. Bake on rack for 10 minutes at 350 degrees until bacon is crisp and sugar slightly caramelized.

Hot Crab Dip

Yield: 1 ½ cups

1 8-ounce package cream cheese, softened
1 tablespoon milk
1 6½-ounce can flaked crabmeat
2 tablespoons finely chopped onion
½ teaspoon cream-style horseradish
¼ teaspoon salt
dash pepper
⅓ cup sliced almonds, toasted

Preheat oven to 375 degrees.
1. Blend all ingredients well.
2. Spoon into small, lightly buttered ovenproof baking dish.
3. Sprinkle with almonds and bake at 375 degrees for 15 minutes. Serve hot with crackers or small rounds of thinly sliced rye bread.

Guacamole Dip

Yield: 1 ½ cups

4 large avocados, finely chopped
1 tablespoon finely chopped onion
2 tablespoons salad oil
1 tablespoon wine vinegar
1 tablespoon lemon juice
¼ teaspoon ground oregano
¼ teaspoon pepper
1 large tomato, finely chopped
dash of garlic powder
salt to taste

Mix all ingredients about 30 minutes before using and season to taste. Will keep overnight if covered tightly.

Eggplant Puffs

Make these ahead for unexpected guests...they're freezable.

Yield: 36-48 puffs

2 medium eggplants
³/₄ cup grated Swiss cheese
1 egg, slightly beaten
2 tablespoons breadcrumbs
¹/₂ teaspoon cumin
¹/₂ teaspoon garlic powder
¹/₂ teaspoon lemon juice
¹/₂ teaspoon salt
¹/₄ teaspoon pepper
1 cup flour
oil for frying

Preheat oven to 350 degrees.
1. Boil eggplant until soft. Let cool and peel.
2. Mash eggplant; add all ingredients, except flour, and mix well.
3. Drop by teaspoonfuls into flour, roll to coat all sides and fry in oil until crisp.
4. Bake at 350 degrees for 15 minutes.

Herring Pâté

Yield: 1¹/₂ cups

1 1-pound jar of pickled herring fillets in wine sauce
2 small pieces of dry bread
2 hard-cooked eggs
1 apple, peeled and cored
1 small onion
sugar to taste

1. Drain liquid off herring. Soak bread in herring liquid till wet throughout. Set aside.
2. Chop herring, eggs, apple and onion together (or put through grinder or food processor).

3. Add soaked bread and mix well; sugar may be added to taste. Serve with dark rye bread or assorted crackers.

 To easily remove the shells from hard-cooked eggs, use salt in the water and quickly rinse them in cold water.

Mexican Dip

Forecast: Chili today—hot tamale!!

Yield: A large platterful

1 10½-ounce can bean dip
3 avocados, mashed
lemon juice
3 small green onions, chopped
4 tablespoons sour cream
4 tablespoons mayonnaise
1 package taco seasonings
4 ounces Monterey Jack cheese, grated
4 ounces Cheddar cheese, grated
3 tomatoes, chopped
1 3-ounce can chopped olives

1. Layer the ingredients on a platter, beginning with the bean dip.
2. Cover that with the avocados, mashed with the lemon juice; then cover with the onions.
3. Mix the sour cream with the mayonnaise and taco seasoning. Spread over the onions.
4. Follow with the cheese, tomatoes, olives and more sour cream on top.
5. Surround with unsalted tostado chips—dip is salty enough.

Danish Meatballs

Golfers will love the high compression!

Yield: 8 servings

3/4 pound ground beef
1/4 pound ground pork
1 small onion, grated
1/2 cup fine dry breadcrumbs
1 teaspoon salt
1/4 teaspoon pepper
1/8 teaspoon nutmeg
1/8 teaspoon marjoram
2 eggs
1/2 cup milk
3 tablespoons shortening
1 10-ounce can condensed consommé

1. Combine beef and pork with onion, breadcrumbs, seasonings, eggs and milk in medium-size bowl; mix lightly with fork.
2. Shape into about 48 small balls.
3. Brown a few at a time in shortening in large skillet. Drain off fat and return meatballs to pan.
4. Add consommé and cover. Simmer 15 minutes or until cooked through. Remove meatballs with slotted spoon. Keep hot. Make sauce.

Sauce

2 tablespoons flour
3 tablespoons water
2 tablespoons sweet relish

1. Pour all liquid from frying pan into a cup. Add water, if needed, to make 1 cup. Return to frying pan and heat to boiling.
2. Blend flour and water. Stir into hot liquid. Cook, stirring constantly, until sauce thickens and boil one minute longer. Stir in sweet relish.

To serve, place meatballs in chafing dish and pour sauce over.

Stuffed Mushrooms

Yield: 24 mushrooms

1 pound large, fresh mushrooms
¼ cup Italian or Caesar dressing
1 cup soft breadcrumbs
¼ cup grated Parmesan cheese
1 tablespoon finely chopped parsley

Preheat oven to 350 degrees.
1. Remove and finely chop mushroom stems.
2. In medium bowl, combine chopped stems, dressing, breadcrumbs, cheese and parsley.
3. Fill each mushroom with breadcrumb mixture; place in shallow baking dish.
4. Add water to barely cover bottom of dish and bake 20 minutes. Serve hot or cold.

Polynesian Appetizer Microwave

Yield: 2 cups

1 tablespoon packed brown sugar
2 teaspoons cornstarch
⅛ teaspoon ground ginger
⅛ teaspoon garlic powder
1 tablespoon water
1 tablespoon soy sauce
1 8¼-ounce can pineapple chunks, drained
    and ⅓ cup juice reserved
8 ounces brown-and-serve sausage

1. In a 1-quart casserole, blend brown sugar, cornstarch, ginger, garlic powder, water, soy sauce and pineapple juice.
2. Cut each sausage into thirds. Stir into casserole with pineapple chunks.
3. Microwave on High 3-7 minutes or until sauce is thickened, stirring 2 or 3 times.
4. Serve with toothpicks and lots of napkins!

Rumaki with Plum Sauce

Yield: 16 pieces

¹/₂ pound chicken livers
1 quart salted water
¹/₂ pound sliced bacon, cut in thirds
1 8-ounce can water chestnuts, each chestnut cut in
  4 slices

1. Boil the chicken livers in salted water until cooked; slice in small pieces.
2. Wrap a piece of bacon around a slice of water chestnut and a piece of liver. Secure with a toothpick.
3. Broil the rumaki until the bacon is cooked. Serve warm with Plum Sauce.

Plum Sauce

4 ounces wild plum jam
juice of ¹/₂ lime
1 small scallion, sliced
dash of salt
good dash of Tabasco sauce

Mix together and heat.

Salmon Mousse

Fit for a winner.

Yield: 2 cups

1 envelope plain gelatin
2 tablespoons lemon juice
1 small onion, sliced
¹/₂ cup boiling water
¹/₂ cup mayonnaise
¹/₄ teaspoon paprika
¹/₄ cup chili sauce
1 teaspoon dill seed
1 16-ounce can salmon
1 cup heavy cream, whipped

1. Empty gelatin into blender, add lemon juice, onion slices and water. Cover blender and blend at high speed.
2. Add mayonnaise, paprika, chili sauce, dill seed and salmon. Blend at high speed.
3. Gently fold in whipped cream.
4. Pour into an oiled mold and chill overnight.
5. Unmold on bed of salad greens and serve with small rounds of thinly sliced rye bread.

Sardine Spread

Direct from Cannery Row.

Yield: 1 ½ cups

1 2-ounce tin skinless and boneless sardines
1 8-ounce package cream cheese
1 tablespoon anchovy paste
1 teaspoon lemon juice
1 teaspoon Worcestershire sauce

Blend all ingredients together in mixer, blender or food processor. Serve with assorted crackers or crudités.

Spiced Shrimp

An interesting variation for shrimp.

Yield: 16-20 shrimp

¼ cup butter
½ teaspoon ground ginger
¼ teaspoon turmeric
1 teaspoon salt
⅛ teaspoon pepper
1 clove garlic, peeled and chopped
1 pound raw shrimp, shelled and deveined

1. Melt butter in large skillet; add spices and garlic.
2. Stir to combine. Add shrimp and sauté 3 to 5 minutes, until done and tender.

Zucchini Appetizer   Kim Novak

Kim knows that good exercise and good food will keep you in great shape. Although Kim does not golf, she practices good nutrition to stay "movie-star fit" This recipe could also be used as a side dish to your entrée.

Yield: About 36 squares

3 cups thinly sliced zucchini
1 cup Bisquick baking mix
1/2 cup grated Parmesan cheese
2 tablespoons chopped parsley
1/2 teaspoon salt
1/2 teaspoon seasoned salt
1/2 teaspoon oregano
1 clove garlic, chopped
1/2 cup vegetable oil
4 eggs, slightly beaten

Preheat oven to 350 degrees.
1. Grease well a 13 × 9 × 2-inch pan.
2. Mix all ingredients together. Spread in pan.
3. Bake until golden brown, about 25 minutes.
4. Cut into squares and pass with drinks.

Eggplant Appetizer Low Fat

This appetizer is even better if made a day ahead.

Yield: 8 servings (25 calories each)

1 large eggplant
1 onion, finely chopped
1 clove garlic, minced
1 large tomato, peeled and finely chopped
3/4 teaspoon salt
1/8 teaspoon freshly ground black pepper
2 teaspoons red wine vinegar
sliced black olives for garnish (optional)

Preheat oven to 400 degrees.
1. Wash the eggplant and pierce the skin in several places. Place the eggplant in a shallow pan and bake in the oven until tender, about 30 minutes.
2. Allow the eggplant to cool until it can be handled easily. Then peel it and chop into very small pieces.
3. Add the remaining ingredients to the eggplant and mix well.
4. Refrigerate the eggplant mixture until thoroughly chilled.
5. Garnish with sliced olives.

Soups

Asparagus and Potato Soup

Yield: 6 servings

1 bunch fresh asparagus
3 medium potatoes, peeled
1 tablespoon butter
2 egg yolks
½ cup heavy cream
nutmeg
whipped cream for garnish

1. Scrape and clean asparagus and cook in very little salted water until almost tender.
2. Remove from the saucepan and using the same water, cook the potatoes. When very soft, mash potatoes and add 6 cups boiling water and the tender part of the asparagus stalks, reserving 6 tips for garnish.
3. Mash the asparagus with a potato masher; simmer for 1 hour.
4. Put the soup through a strainer and stir in the butter.
5. Before serving, remove from heat and gradually stir in the egg yolks beaten with the heavy cream.
6. Heat soup, but do not boil, stirring constantly. Season to taste.
7. Serve in cups with asparagus tips for garnish, nutmeg and 1 teaspoon whipped cream, if desired.

Cold Avocado Soup

An elegant ritual.

Yield: 6 servings

1 10¾-ounce can cream of chicken soup
1 cup clam juice
¾ cup puréed avocado (2-3 avocados)
2 tablespoons sherry
dash of pepper
¾ cup chilled cream
lemon slices for garnish

1. Combine soup and clam juice in pan; heat and stir until smooth.
2. Remove from heat and stir in avocado purée, sherry and pepper.
3. Chill. Just before serving, stir in cream.
4. Float lemon slices on each serving.

Black Bean Soup

You'll want seconds!

Yield: 2½ quarts

2½ quarts boiling water
2 cups dried black beans
1 tomato, chopped
1 green pepper, seeded and chopped
1 celery stalk, chopped
1 large onion, chopped
1 tablespoon parsley
¼ teaspoon ground cloves
¼ teaspoon savory
2 tablespoons arrowroot
¼ cup skim milk

1. Without disturbing the boil, add the beans slowly to boiling water.

2. Reduce heat and simmer for 2 hours. Add vegetables and spices and continue simmering 10 more minutes.
3. Make a paste of the arrowroot and milk. Bring the soup to a boil.
4. Add paste and simmer 10 minutes more.

Herbed Lima Bean Soup

Yield: 8 servings

1 pound dried baby lima beans
water
1 16-ounce can whole tomatoes, broken up
¼ cup instant minced onion
2 teaspoons marjoram leaves
¼ teaspoon ground black pepper
1 bay leaf
1 cup sliced carrots
1 cup sliced celery
2½ teaspoons salt

1. In a large saucepot, place the lima beans. Cover with boiling water; let stand for 1 hour.
2. Add 8 cups water, tomatoes, onion, 1½ teaspoons of the marjoram, black pepper, and bay leaf. Bring to a boil. Reduce heat and simmer, covered, until the beans are tender, about 1½ hours.
3. Add the carrots, celery, salt and the remaining marjoram, crushed. Simmer, covered, until the vegetables are tender, about 10 minutes.
4. Remove the bay leaf before serving.

 Add a finely grated raw carrot to vegetable soups before serving; it gives a rich color and adds flavor and texture.

Senate Bean Soup

Try this tempting, different taste treat.

Yield: 6-8 servings

2 cups small navy beans
water
1 smoked ham hock
1 medium potato, peeled and finely chopped
1 onion, chopped
½ cup chopped celery
1 clove garlic, minced
salt and pepper
parsley for garnish

1. Soak beans overnight in 1 quart water.
2. Drain beans and measure water, adding enough water to make 2 quarts.
3. Place beans, water and ham hock in kettle; cover and simmer for 2 hours. Add potato, onion, celery and garlic. Simmer 1 hour. Remove ham hock and cut up meat. Remove 1 cup of beans and some liquid and purée in blender.
4. Return meat and beans to soup. Heat. Season to taste. Garnish with parsley.

Blender Borscht

Blazing intensity of color!

Yield: 5-6 servings

1 cup sour cream
1 16-ounce can diced beets, chilled and drained
½ slice lemon, peeled
½ small onion, sliced
½ teaspoon salt
½ teaspoon sugar
1 cup crushed ice

1. In blender, add ¾ cup sour cream, beets, lemon, onion, salt and sugar.
2. Cover and blend at high speed about 15 seconds. Scrape down sides of container; add ice. Cover and blend about 10 seconds longer.
3. Serve immediately, topped with dollops of remaining sour cream.

Spiced Cherry Hungarian Borscht

Flamboyant!! Best if made a day in advance.

Yield: 4-6 servings

1 pound sweet red cherries
rind of ½ lemon
6 whole cloves
1 3-inch stick cinnamon
⅓ cup sugar
½ teaspoon salt
3 cups water
2 teaspoons quick cooking tapioca
1 cup red wine
thin lemon slices for garnish
sour cream for garnish

1. Wash cherries and remove stems and pits.
2. Remove rind from lemon in strips, using vegetable peeler.
3. Stick cloves into rind. Simmer, uncovered, the cherries, lemon rind with cloves, cinnamon and sugar, salt and water, for about 15 minutes.
4. Stir in tapioca gradually. Bring to a boil, then remove from heat. Stir in wine and allow to cool. Remove and discard lemon rind, cloves and cinnamon. Refrigerate.
5. Serve ice cold, topping each serving with lemon slices and dollop of sour cream.

Cream of Broccoli Soup

Bill Sander

Bill is a straight shooter from Seattle. He turned professional in 1977 and was a member of the Walker Cup Team that year. Before that, he won the 1976 United States Amateur Championship. He recommends you do not salt this recipe. You will enjoy the smooth texture of this soup.

Yield: 4 servings

1 bunch fresh broccoli
1 medium onion, chopped
2 14½-ounce cans chicken broth
3 tablespoons butter or margarine
3 tablespoons flour
1 pint half & half
paprika and pepper to taste*

1. Cook broccoli and onion in chicken broth until tender.
2. While this is cooking, melt butter in small skillet and add flour to make roux. Cook on medium heat for 2-3 minutes, stirring often.
3. When broccoli is tender, use potato masher to mash it; return to medium heat and stir in roux. Stir continuously. Add half & half to thickness desired.

   *DO NOT SALT.

Bouillabaisse (The Fisherman's Stew)

Hearty and robust!! A Cajun delight. (See photograph)

Yield: 4 servings

1/2 cup chopped onion
1 clove garlic, minced
1/2 cup chopped celery
1 carrot, sliced
1 green pepper, chopped
1 yellow pepper, chopped (optional)
2 large, fresh tomatoes, chopped
1/4 cup olive oil
1 8-ounce can tomato sauce
1 teaspoon salt
2 to 3 teaspoons paprika
pinch of dried basil
3 bay leaves
1/2 cup white wine
2 cups water
1 pound medium or large shrimp
2 to 3 halibut steaks, cut in 1-inch pieces
12 mussels
1 Dungeness crab
chopped chives and parsley for garnish

1. Sauté onions, garlic, celery, carrots, peppers and
   tomatoes in oil until light brown.
2. Add tomato sauce, seasonings, wine and water. Simmer
   for 20 minutes.
3. Add remaining ingredients and seafood and simmer 5 to
   6 minutes.
4. Remove bay leaves. Garnish and serve hot.

Quick Crab Bisque

Yield: 6-8 servings

1 10½-ounce can tomato soup
1 15-ounce can green pea soup
1 14½-ounce can consommé
1 soup can milk
salt and pepper to taste
dash of Worcestershire sauce
2 6-ounce packages frozen Alaska crabmeat, thawed
    and drained
2 tablespoons sherry

1. About 20 minutes before serving, mix together tomato soup, pea soup, consommé, milk, salt, pepper and Worcestershire sauce.
2. Simmer for 10 minutes over low heat. Then add the crabmeat and simmer for 10 more minutes.
3. Just before serving, stir in the sherry.

♀ Were you heavy handed with the salt when making soup? A cut-up or whole potato will fix it up!

Cucumber Soup

Yield: 4 servings

3 cucumbers
¼ cup butter
2 onions, finely chopped
1 bay leaf
1 teaspoon salt
1 tablespoon flour
3 cups water
1 cup half & half
2 tablespoons lemon juice
½ teaspoon dill weed
¼ cup Chablis
sour cream

1. Pare cucumbers. Slice 2 of them finely and sauté in the butter along with the chopped onion, bay leaf and salt.
2. When cucumbers are soft and golden, blend in the flour. Add the water and simmer, covered, about 30 minutes. Chill well. Skim off any fat.
3. Cut the remaining cucumber down the middle and scoop out the seeds. Grate into the chilled soup. Add half & half, lemon juice, dill weed and Chablis.
4. Serve in chilled cups with a dollop of sour cream.

Swedish Fruit Soup   Microwave

It's a dessert or a breakfast dish. Serve either hot or cold.

Yield: 6-8 servings

1 12-ounce package mixed dried fruit
1 12-ounce package dried apricots
¹/₂ cup raisins
¹/₂ lemon, thinly sliced
2 quarts water
1 cup sugar
2 tablespoons quick-cooking tapioca
¹/₂ teaspoon salt
3 cinnamon sticks

1. Combine mixed fruits, apricots, raisins, lemon slices, and water in a 3-quart glass casserole.
2. Stir in sugar, tapioca, salt, and cinnamon sticks.
3. Microwave on High, covered, for about 15 minutes or until boiling.
4. Microwave on Medium for 25 minutes longer, or until fruits are tender.

Chilled Melon Soup   Microwave

A summertime favorite.

Yield: 4 servings

1 large cantaloupe
3 tablespoons butter
1 tablespoon sugar
grated rind and juice of ½ lemon
dash of ginger
dash of ground mace
½ teaspoon salt
2 cups water
⅔ cup white wine
few sprigs of mint for garnish

1. Cut the melon in half and discard the seeds. Scoop a few melon balls from the flesh and set aside for garnish.
2. Remove and dice all the remaining melon flesh; place in a large, deep casserole with the butter, sugar, lemon rind and juice, ginger, mace, and salt. Microwave on High for 5 minutes.
3. Purée the mixture in an electric blender. Stir in the water and wine and chill in the refrigerator for 2 to 3 hours.
4. Add more salt and pepper, if desired; turn into a serving tureen or individual soup bowls. Serve chilled, garnish with the melon and sprigs of mint.

Minestrone Soup

A skillful manipulation of flavors.

Yield: 8 servings

⅓ cup salad or olive oil
¼ cup butter or margarine
1 large onion, diced
3 large carrots, diced
2 stalks celery, diced
2 potatoes, peeled and diced
½ pound green beans, cut into 1-inch pieces
6 cups water
1 small head cabbage, shredded
1 16-ounce can tomatoes
2 medium zucchini, diced
6 beef-flavored bouillon cubes
1 teaspoon salt
1 16-ounce can white kidney beans, drained
1 16-ounce can red kidney beans, drained
½ cup Parmesan cheese

1. In large saucepot heat oil and butter. Cook onions, carrots, celery, potatoes and green beans until vegetables are lightly browned, about 20 minutes.
2. Add water, cabbage, tomatoes with their liquid, zucchini, bouillon cubes and salt. Heat to boiling, breaking up the tomatoes.
3. Reduce heat and cover; simmer for 40 minutes or until all the vegetables are very tender. *Do not overcook!*
4. Stir in beans; cook another 15 minutes until the soup thickens.
5. Pass cheese separately to sprinkle individually.

Mushroom Soup   Jan Stephenson

Jan hails from Sydney, Australia and looks as beautiful in the kitchen as on the course. This soup is a complete meal with a green salad and sourdough bread. It's a delight for luncheon or light supper.

Yield: 4-6 servings

5 tablespoons oil
1 ½ pounds mushrooms
4 stalks celery
1 large onion
1 can tuna, drained
¼ cup soy sauce
6 cups milk
1 tablespoon butter
4 tablespoons flour
salt and pepper

1. Finely chop mushrooms, celery and onion and simmer in oil until soft. Leave simmering.
2. In soup pot, heat milk, soy sauce and tuna. Leave simmering.
3. After vegetables are cooked, add butter and flour. (Add flour slowly to avoid lumps.)
4. Add salt and pepper to taste.
5. Add to milk solution and cook on very low heat for 1 hour or until it thickens.
6. Stir occasionally; add more soy sauce if needed.

French Onion Soup   Jim Burke

Jim plays out of the Champion Golf Club in Houston, Texas. This soup is a real classic. Jim suggests you can add 1 teaspoon of cognac to each bowl before adding the cheese.

Yield: 8 servings

3 quarts water
½ pound beef knuckles
½ pound suet
6 carrots, chopped
6 stalks celery, chopped
3 or 4 leeks, chopped
8 large onions
1 tablespoon olive oil
croutons
Gruyère cheese

1. In water, boil beef knuckles, suet, carrots, celery and leeks. Cook for 2 hours; spoon off grease and strain.
2. Cut up onions into thin slices; separate and cook to a golden brown color in large pot with olive oil.
3. Put onions into stock. Cook for 1 more hour.
4. Spoon soup into oven-type soup bowls. Cover with croutons and Gruyère cheese. Broil in oven till cheese is melted.
5. Serve immediately with French bread and red wine.

Hearty Creamy Potato Soup

We all know it never rains on the golf course—but this tastes great after a downpour!

Yield: 4 servings

6 slices bacon, chopped
1 cup chopped onion
2 cups cubed potatoes
1 cup water
1 teaspoon salt
2 10¾-ounce cans cream of mushroom soup
2 soup cans milk
2 tablespoons parsley, chopped

1. In a saucepan, cook bacon until crisp; set bacon aside.
2. Pour off all but 3 tablespoons fat; add onions and brown.
3. Add potatoes and water. Cook, covered, 15 minutes or until potatoes are tender. Stir in salt, soup and milk.
4. Heat, but do not boil. Garnish with parsley and bacon.

Cold Raspberry Soup

Beautiful and delicate.

Yield: 6 cups

4 10-ounce packages frozen raspberries, thawed
2 cups port wine
4 cinnamon sticks
2 teaspoons cornstarch
½ cup water

1. In a 3-quart saucepan over medium heat, heat raspberries, port and cinnamon sticks to boiling. Reduce heat to low and simmer 10 minutes.
2. In small bowl mix cornstarch with water. Slowly stir into soup; cook until thickened. Cover and refrigerate. Before serving, remove cinnamon sticks.

Sopa de Tortilla John Mahaffey

This recipe is from John's mother and is one of his favorites. Since they live in Texas, John and his wife, Susie, often serve Mexican cuisine to friends and family.

Yield: 6 generous servings

meat from 1 cooked chicken
1 10¾-ounce can cream of mushroom soup
1 10¾-ounce can cream of chicken soup
1 medium onion, diced and sautéed
garlic salt
salt and pepper to taste
1 cup grated sharp cheese
1 dozen corn tortillas, torn or cut into pieces

Preheat oven to 350 degrees.
1. Mix above ingredients, except for cheese and tortillas, in a bowl.
2. Place a layer of tortillas in casserole dish.
3. Spread a layer of soup mixture on top. Sprinkle with cheese.

4. Add another layer of tortillas, soup and cheese.
5. Layer until all is used up; top with cheese.
6. Bake at 350 degrees for 1 hour. Allow casserole to set a few minutes before serving.

It can be made ahead of time and even frozen, but the cooking time may need to be increased slightly. It should be very bubbly after it cooks.

Zucchini Bisque   Chris Roderick

Chris is the golf professional at the prestigious Olympic Club in San Francisco, and this recipe is in the elegant tradition of San Francisco cuisine. For best results, make this appealing soup one day ahead.

Yield: 4 servings

2 medium onions, diced
¹/₂ cup butter
8-10 medium zucchini, sliced
1 10¹/₂-ounce can chicken broth
1 ¹/₂ cups cream or half & half
sour cream
nutmeg
fresh chives

1. Sauté onions in butter until soft; add sliced zucchini and chicken broth.
2. Cover and allow to simmer 12-15 minutes until zucchini is done. Allow to cool.
3. Place in blender and add cream and mix.
4. Pour in small bowls, top with spoonful of sour cream, dash of nutmeg and freshly chopped chives.

Provençal Fish Soup Low Fat

Yield: 4 servings (277 calories each)

1 large onion, finely chopped
2 whole cloves garlic
1 carrot, sliced
¼ cup chopped green pepper
2 tablespoons olive oil
2 cups fish stock
pinch saffron
1 bay leaf
1 tablespoon lemon juice
2 medium tomatoes, finely chopped
1 pound halibut, cut up
1 dozen clams
½ cup shrimp, peeled
salt and pepper to taste

1. Sauté onions, garlic, carrots, and pepper in oil until light brown.
2. Add fish stock and seasonings. Simmer for 20 minutes.
3. Add remaining ingredients and simmer 5 to 6 minutes.
4. Remove bay leaf and garlic and serve warm.

Cabbage Soup Low Fat

Yield: 5 servings (21 calories each)

1 cup finely chopped onion
1 medium tomato, chopped
¼ green pepper, minced
1 teaspoon salt
¼ teaspoon pepper
½ teaspoon caraway seeds
2 cups beef stock
2 teaspoons garlic vinegar
1 teaspoon sugar
3 cups cabbage, shredded
3 cups cold water

1. Place onion, tomato, green pepper, salt, pepper and caraway seed with 2 cups stock in large pot.
2. Bring to a boil, reduce heat and let simmer for 20 minutes.
3. Add vinegar, sugar, cabbage and 3 cups cold water.
4. Bring to a boil and cook for 10 to 12 minutes.

Salads and Dressings

Antipasto Salad   Mrs. Bob Hope

"This can be served as a first course salad or even as a main dish," Dolores Hope suggests.

Yield: 6-8 servings

1 head iceberg lettuce (very cold and dry)
olives, ripe, drained and chilled
pimento, drained and chilled
Genovese salami, cut in slivers
garbanzo beans, drained and chilled
Mozzarella cheese, diced
Romano cheese, grated
marinated artichoke hearts, chilled
mild Italian peppers, pickled, drained
celery hearts and tops, very finely chopped

Salad Dressing

vinegar and oil, approximately 3 parts oil to 1 part vinegar
coarsely ground pepper and salt

1. Arrange bed of lettuce greens in chilled salad bowl and top with above ingredients (excluding dressing).
2. Bring it to the table untossed to show off the colorful arrangement.
3. Add salt, pepper and vinegar and toss lightly. Add oil and toss again.
4. Serve with hot crusty bread.

Apple Salad with Honey Peanut Dressing   Terry Diehl

Winner of the 1974 San Antonio, Texas Open, Terry and his family live in Rochester, New York. "This salad is a real favorite with our family, which includes four sons." Casual entertaining, with flexible menus, is the style for Terry's and Marci's growing family.

Yield: 6-8 servings

Salad

4 crisp apples
½ cup raisins
2-3 stalks celery, chopped or
1 ½ cups sliced green grapes
1 cup chopped peanuts

Dressing

¼ cup honey
⅓ cup peanut butter
½ cup mayonnaise

1. Peel, slice and chop apples into bite-sized pieces.
2. Add raisins, celery or grapes and chopped peanuts.
3. For dressing, blend together honey, peanut butter and mayonnaise until creamy.
4. Toss salad ingredients gently, then add dressing and toss again. Make just before serving.

Caesar Salad   DeeDee Lasker

A golfer since she was 12, DeeDee has enjoyed a successful amateur and collegiate career. When not on tour, she enjoys jogging, tennis, basketball and eating good, nutritious food to stay in shape.

Yield: 4-6 servings

2 cloves garlic, crushed
1 teaspoon salt
1 coddled egg
6 tablespoons olive oil
2 tablespoons wine vinegar
1 tablespoon fresh lemon juice
½ teaspoon Worcestershire sauce
1 teaspoon dry mustard
½ teaspoon salt
1 teaspoon coarsely ground black pepper
4 fillets of anchovies, cut in small pieces
1 tablespoon grated Parmesan cheese
½ head crisp Romaine lettuce
croutons

1. Into a large wooden salad bowl place garlic cloves and salt. Crush the garlic pieces with a fork and rub in bowl until bowl is well flavored with garlic.
2. Add the coddled egg.
3. Add oil and beat rapidly with fork until thick, about 1 minute. Then add wine vinegar and lemon juice, slowly, and beat until blended well with oil.
4. Add Worcestershire sauce, dry mustard, salt, pepper, anchovies and Parmesan cheese. Beat until well blended.
5. Add lettuce and toss.
6. Add the croutons, toss again.

 Dry mustard rubbed on your hands prior to rinsing them in cold water will eliminate onion and garlic smell.

Caesar Supreme   John Joseph

"A green for all seasons." John serves as golf professional at Green Hills Country Club, Millbrae, California. This is his favorite salad for hot-weather luncheons.

Yield: 4 servings

2 heads Romaine lettuce
a few anchovies
1/3 cup olive oil
1 clove garlic, chopped
3 teaspoons red wine vinegar
3 teaspoons Worcestershire sauce
pinch dry mustard
1 egg yolk
juice of 1/2 lemon
few drops of Tabasco sauce
Parmesan cheese, grated
croutons

1. Clean, wash and break the lettuce and chill.
2. Use a wooden bowl and rub entire bowl with anchovies. Discard excess anchovies.
3. Coat bowl with olive oil until it pools in bottom of bowl.
4. Add garlic, vinegar, Worcestershire sauce, mustard, egg yolk, lemon juice, and Tabasco. Mix all together, then add cheese until mixture has the consistency of hot oatmeal. Add lettuce and croutons and mix together well.
5. Serve on ice cold plates with cold forks.
6. Add freshly ground pepper to top of salad, if desired.

Favorite Chicken Salad
George Burns III

A favorite from a favorite. George and his wife, Irene, love to travel and visit interesting places. They have many mementos from places they have been. This salad is a luncheon dish they enjoy when they are home in Florida.

Yield: 6 servings

2 cups water
1 medium onion, sliced (white or yellow)
4 large chicken breasts, skinned and boned
   (approximately 2 ¹/₂ pounds)
1 tablespoon chopped parsley
¹/₂ tablespoon Fine Herbs (McCormick brand)
cracked pepper to taste
1 green bell pepper, chopped
3 spring onions, chopped
3 stalks celery, chopped
¹/₄ cup milk
1 cup mayonnaise

1. In large frying pan, heat water to boiling.
2. Lower to slow boil, add sliced onion and chicken breasts. Cook 30 minutes; turn, add parsley, Fine Herbs, and pepper.
3. Cook an additional 30 minutes. Remove chicken from pan, drain and cool. Discard water and onion.
4. When chicken is cooled, cube it into bite-sized pieces and place in serving bowl. Add pepper, onion and celery; mix well.
5. Add milk and mayonnaise; mix well. Cover and chill.

 Best if prepared in morning for cool, light supper; or night before for luncheon.

Attractive served for a luncheon on rings of cantaloupe.

Hot Chicken Salad

Yield: 4-6 servings

½ cup slivered almonds
2 cups cooked diced chicken *
1 cup chopped celery
1 cup mayonnaise
1 small onion, grated
1 cup grated Cheddar cheese

Preheat oven to 350 degrees.
1. Reserve ¼ cup almonds for topping. Mix remaining ingredients in bowl.
2. Pour into greased casserole and top with reserved almonds. Bake at 350 degrees for 30 minutes.

   *May use boneless chicken breasts.

Microwave Coleslaw   Microwave

So quick and easy.

Yield: 3 cups

2 pounds cabbage, shredded
¾ cup oil
½ cup white vinegar
¼ cup sugar
¼ cup honey
1 teaspoon salt

1. Arrange cabbage in large mixing bowl.
2. Combine oil, vinegar, sugar, honey and salt in a 3-quart saucepan or microwave-safe bowl.
3. Bring mixture to a rolling boil in microwave oven—about 3 minutes. Immediately pour vinegar mixture over cabbage. Chill until ready to serve.

Fruit Salad with Dressing

Brad Bryant

Brad was born in Texas and lives with his wife, Sue, in Orlando, Florida. They recommend you try this salad. The dressing makes it very special. A real contender on the tour, Brad enjoys fishing and hunting for a change of pace from golf.

Yield: 4-6 servings

3 tablespoons margarine
3 tablespoons flour
1 cup sugar
juice from a 20-ounce can pineapple chunks or slices
2 eggs, beaten
1 fresh pineapple, cut into slices
4 sliced bananas
other fruit, if desired

1. Melt margarine. Stir in flour and sugar. Add pineapple juice and stir.
2. Add beaten eggs and cook in double boiler over very low heat, stirring until quite thick.
3. Mix with fruit; serve on large lettuce leaves.

Jicama Excabeche Tim Norris

Winner of the 1982 Sammy Davis, Jr. Greater Hartford Open with a blistering 27-under-par 257, Tim now lives in Texas. He is fond of this unusual Spanish-style salad, perfect for a summer buffet. The blending of the spices gives it a pickled flavor. Best served on chilled plates.

Yield: 2½ quarts

3-4 carrots
salted water
1 cup vinegar
1 cup water
½ cup oil
3 onions, sliced
6 cloves garlic
1 teaspoon salt
2 teaspoons oregano
3-4 bay leaves
1 4-ounce can jalapeño chilies
2 large jicamas, peeled and sliced

1. Cut carrots into small chunks, cook in salted water until almost tender. Drain and cool.
2. In a large pot, combine vinegar, water, oil, onions, garlic, and salt and cook until onions are almost tender.
3. Add oregano and bay leaves. Boil and let cool. Add carrots, jalapeños*, and jicamas; let sit for several hours. Store in refrigerator. Remove bay leaves before serving. Can be served as a salad or appetizer.

   *For milder flavor, cut down on the jalapeños.

24-Hour Lettuce Salad

D. A. Weibring

This salad tastes as good as it looks. D.A. is one of the most colorful players on the PGA tour. He plays out of the beautiful Shipyard Plantation, Hilton Head Island, South Carolina. He and his wife, Kristy, like to serve this salad in a glass bowl to show off the colors.

Yield: 6-8 servings

1 large head iceberg lettuce
1/2 cup chopped green onions
1/2 cup chopped green pepper
1 cup chopped celery
1 10-ounce package frozen peas; leave frozen
2 cups mayonnaise
1/2 to 1 cup Parmesan cheese, grated
2 tablespoons sugar
1 pound bacon, fried crisp and crumbled

1. Layer first 5 ingredients, starting with the lettuce and ending with the frozen peas.
2. Spread the mayonnaise on top.
3. Sprinkle generously with cheese and sugar.
4. Top with the bacon.
5. Toss right before serving.

Rice and Artichoke Salad

Amy Alcott

When Amy leaves the tour, she heads for the kitchen. She loves to cook and, sometimes, in her off-time, works as a short-order cook! Amy passed the magic Million Dollar Mark in 1983. This salad is one of her favorites.

Yield: 6 servings

1 6-ounce package chicken-flavored rice mix
4 green onions, thinly sliced
1/2 cup chopped green pepper
12 pimento-stuffed olives, sliced, or
1 2-ounce jar pimentos
2 6-ounce jars marinated artichoke hearts
3/4 teaspoon curry powder
1/3 cup mayonnaise (may use less, if desired)

1. Cook rice as directed on package, omitting butter. Cool in a large bowl.
2. Add onions, green pepper and olives. Drain artichoke hearts, reserving marinade and halve the artichokes.
3. Combine artichoke marinade with curry powder and mayonnaise.
4. Add artichoke hearts to rice salad and toss with dressing. Chill.

Spinach Salad

The finest of greens. Prepare the dressing ahead of time to enhance its flavor.

Yield: 6-8 servings

Salad

2 pounds fresh spinach
1 large red onion
2 8-ounce cans water chestnuts
4 hard-cooked eggs
1 16-ounce can bean sprouts

Dressing

1 cup salad oil ← CANOLA or OLIVE
¾ cup sugar
1 teaspoon Worcestershire sauce
⅓ cup wine vinegar
2 teaspoons salt
⅓ cup catsup DEL MONTE
2 cloves garlic, minced

1. Wash, drain and remove stems of spinach; tear spinach into bite-sized pieces.
2. Peel and slice the onion; separate into rings.
3. Slice the water chestnuts and eggs. Rinse the bean sprouts in water and drain.
4. Combine all ingredients in large bowl.
5. Mix the dressing and add to the salad.

Shrimp Romaine

A very interesting starter.

Yield: 8 servings

1 cup sour cream
1 cup mayonnaise
2 teaspoons sugar
pinch of salt
2 hard-cooked eggs, chopped
6 sweet gherkins, chopped
½ small onion, grated
½ clove garlic, minced
3-4 teaspoons pickle juice
½ bottle chili sauce
lemon juice to taste
2 pounds shrimp, cooked

1. Mix all ingredients for sauce together.
2. Add shrimp.
3. Refrigerate overnight. Serve with dark bread.

Turkish Chef's Salad

Yield: 1-2 servings

1 cup crisp shredded lettuce
1/2 medium tomato, diced
1/2 medium cucumber, diced
1/2 medium green pepper, diced
2 hard-cooked eggs, sliced
1/2 tablespoon capers

Put all ingredients in large bowl and add dressing.

Dressing

1/2 cup eggplant dressing (see recipe p. 57)
1 tablespoon mayonnaise
1 teaspoon lemon juice

1. Combine these ingredients together and mix well.
2. Pour over salad.

French Salad Dressing
Ralph Landrum

Ralph's interest in golf started when he was ten years old, caddying for his mother and father. Although he played high school basketball, he went to the University of Kentucky on a golf scholarship. His wife, Mary Pat, strongly urges using Miracle Whip (rather than mayonnaise) for this recipe. If you do use regular mayonnaise, it alters the flavor of the dressing and simply "doesn't taste as good!"

1 cup Miracle Whip
½ cup Wesson oil -- OLIVE OR CANOLA
½ cup vinegar - WINE - OR RICEWINE
⅔ cup catsup - DEL MONTE
1 cup sugar
1 tablespoon minced garlic
little salt and pepper

Mix ingredients together and beat.

Eggplant Dressing

An elegant way to spruce up a salad.

Yield: 1 cup

1 small eggplant
½ teaspoon salt
¼ teaspoon pepper
¾ teaspoon lemon juice
dash red hot sauce or powdered ginger, optional

Preheat oven to 400 degrees.
1. Wash eggplant, discard green end, and bake whole on a shallow pan at 400 degrees until it is soft to the touch at its broadest end, about 30 minutes.
2. Cool cooked eggplant, then cut in half lengthwise and scoop flesh from shell.
3. Discard skin and excess seeds.
4. Put the pulp in a bowl and beat it to a purée, using a beater or blender. Stir in seasonings, continuing to beat into a creamy mixture. Store in refrigerator until ready to use.

Variation

Just before using, stir in 1 tablespoon very finely chopped onion per ¼ cup minced celery. Add 1 tablespoon mayonnaise or vegetable oil.

Anchovy French Dressing

Will turn any salad into a happening.

Yield: 4-6 servings

1 2-ounce tin anchovy fillets (rolled with capers), oil included
½ cup cooking oil
½ cup olive oil
1 teaspoon Dijon mustard
1 medium onion, chopped
¼ cup tarragon vinegar

Liquefy in blender or food processor.

Tomato Aspic   Low Fat

A good filler.

Yield: 4 servings (29 calories each)

1½ cups tomato juice
1 teaspoon lemon juice
2 teaspoons minced parsley
½ teaspoon onion powder
¼ teaspoon salt
pinch of pepper
1 tablespoon unflavored gelatin
¼ cup cold water
1 cup mixed greens

1. Heat tomato juice, lemon juice, parsley, onion powder, salt and pepper.
2. Dissolve gelatin in ¼ cup cold water and add to hot tomato juice mixture. Stir well.
3. Pour into 4 individual molds and chill until firm. Serve on bed of greens.

OOOOOOOOOOOOOOOOOOOO

Bread

OOOOOOOOOOOOOOOOOO

Banana Nut Bread Fuzzy Zoeller

Winner of the 1979 Masters Tournament and the 1984
United States Open, Frank Urban Zoeller ranks with the all-
time colorful personalities in the game and his superb
talent keeps his name in the headlines. Headlining his day,
says his wife, Dianna, is Fuzzy's favorite nut bread.

Yield: 1 loaf

½ cup butter
1 cup sugar
2 eggs, beaten
1 teaspoon baking soda
½ cup chopped nuts
2 cups sifted flour
3 mashed bananas

Preheat oven to 350 degrees.
1. Cream butter and sugar.
2. Add beaten eggs, then flour and baking soda.
3. Add bananas and nuts and turn into greased and floured
   9 × 5-inch loaf pan.
4. Bake at 350 degrees for 50-60 minutes.

Bran Muffins   Tom Purtzer

Great for a quick breakfast before a round of golf. Tom is one of the PGA's long drivers, with a smooth, powerful swing. He and his wife, Jacque, like casual entertaining and enjoy these muffins for brunch or lunch.

Yield: 12 muffins

4 teaspoons oil
1 egg
1/2 cup cream
1/2 cup water
3 teaspoons honey
1 cup chopped dates
1 cup flour
1 cup bran flakes cereal
2 teaspoons baking powder
1/2 teaspoon salt
2 teaspoons cinnamon

Preheat oven to 400 degrees.
1. Mix together oil, egg, cream, water and honey.
2. Mix in dates and let them soak for a few minutes while mixing dry ingredients.
3. Mix together flour, bran flakes, baking powder, salt and cinnamon.
4. Stir dry ingredients into date mixture, until just mixed.
5. Fill greased muffin tins 2/3 full and bake at 400 degrees about* 15 minutes.

   *Do not overbake as each oven is different.

 Sticky dates, figs, or raisins will come apart easily if you put them in the oven for a few minutes.

Refrigerator Bran Muffins

Scoop out the dough as needed.

Yield: About 60 muffins

3 cups Kellogg's Bran Buds
1 cup boiling water
1 1/2 cups sugar, granulated
1/2 cup Crisco shortening
2 eggs
2 1/2 cups flour
2 1/2 teaspoons baking soda
1/2 teaspoon salt
2 cups buttermilk

Preheat oven to 400 degrees.
1. In a large bowl, place 3 cups of Bran Buds. Pour boiling water over and mix well with a spoon; set aside.
2. Using electric mixer, mix together sugar and shortening, blending well.
3. Add eggs, one at a time.
4. Mix flour, soda and salt and add to egg mixture alternately with buttermilk; mix until smooth.
5. Add bran mixture, mixing well. (If desired, add dates, nuts, raisins, etc.)
6. Pour into greased muffin tins and bake at 400 degrees for 20 to 25 minutes.

 This dough keeps well: up to 5 weeks in the refrigerator. Use covered plastic container; do not stir, just scoop out and place in greased pan and bake as directed.

French bread, rolls and muffins can be restored to fresh-baked if you place them in a brown paper bag with a half teaspoon of water and heat them in the oven or microwave.

Butterflake Rolls   Johnny Miller

What a great way to get your morning off to a glorious start! Johnny Miller is a dedicated family man as well as a super golfer. He lives in Utah with his wife and six children and is involved in golf course architecture and design, as well as winning tournaments.

Yield: 24 rolls

1 cup scalded milk
1/2 cup sugar
1/2 cup butter
1 tablespoon yeast
1/4 cup warm water
3 eggs
4 cups flour
1 teaspoon salt

Preheat oven to 350 degrees.
1. Combine milk, sugar and butter.
2. Dissolve yeast in warm water. Combine with milk mixture.
3. Beat eggs and add to milk mixture. Mix in flour and salt. This makes a sticky dough. Let rise 5-6 hours or overnight in refrigerator.
4. Roll out in oblong shape on floured board (about 12 × 20 inches). Spread with melted butter. Fold in from each side to make 3 thicknesses. Cut into 24 strips. Wrap around finger and place in greased muffin tins.
5. Let rise 2-3 hours.
6. Bake at 350 degrees for 15 minutes.

Three "C" Bread

Colorful—especially at holiday time. A great hostess gift.

Yield: 4 small loaves

3 eggs, beaten
1/2 cup cooking oil
1/2 cup milk
2 1/2 cups sifted all-purpose flour
1 cup sugar
1 teaspoon baking powder
1 teaspoon baking soda
1 teaspoon cinnamon
1/2 teaspoon salt
2 cups shredded carrots
1 3 1/2-ounce can flaked coconut
1/2 cup snipped maraschino cherries
1/2 cup raisins
1/2 cup pecans, chopped

Preheat oven to 350 degrees.
1. Combine eggs, oil and milk in large bowl. Sift together flour, sugar, baking powder, baking soda, cinnamon and salt.
2. Add to egg mixture; mix just till thoroughly combined.
3. Stir in carrots, coconut, cherries, raisins and pecans.
4. Turn into 4 well-greased and floured 16-ounce fruit or vegetable cans.
5. Bake in 350-degree oven for 45 to 50 minutes.
6. Remove from cans and cool thoroughly.
7. Wrap and refrigerate overnight or until used.

Jalapeño Cornbread   Doug Sanders

This recipe looks as sharp as the donor. One of the tour's free spirits and flashy dressers for more than two decades, Doug has 20 PGA tour victories and is now making a mark in the senior tour.

Yield: 2 loaves

2 ½ cups cornmeal
1 cup flour
2 tablespoons sugar
1 tablespoon salt
4 teaspoons baking powder
3 eggs, lightly beaten
1 ½ cups milk
½ cup cooking oil
1 16-ounce can cream-style corn
2 jalapeño peppers, seeded and chopped
2 cups sharp Cheddar cheese, grated
1 onion, grated

Preheat oven to 425 degrees.
1. In a bowl, combine first 5 ingredients. Mix eggs, milk and oil; add to the cornmeal mixture.
2. Stir in the remaining ingredients and pour into 2 well-greased 9 × 5-inch baking pans.
3. Bake at 425 degrees for 25 minutes or until cooked through.

Cranberry Muffins

An interesting way to use cranberries.

Yield: 18 muffins

2 cups flour
1 cup sugar
1 1/2 teaspoons baking powder
1/2 teaspoon baking soda
2 teaspoons grated orange peel
1 1/2 teaspoons nutmeg
1 teaspoon cinnamon
1/2 teaspoon ginger
1/2 cup shortening
3/4 cup orange juice
1 tablespoon vanilla extract
2 eggs, slightly beaten
1 1/2 cups cranberries
1 1/2 cups chopped walnuts

Preheat oven to 350 degrees.
1. In medium bowl, mix flour, sugar, baking powder, baking soda, orange peel, nutmeg, cinnamon and ginger.
2. Cut in shortening with pastry blender or two knives. Stir in juice, vanilla and eggs. Fold in cranberries and walnuts.
3. Spoon into 18 well-greased or paper-lined muffin cups.
4. Bake in 350-degree oven for 25 minutes or until golden. Serve warm.

English Muffin Loaves   Microwave

Difficult to resist.

Yield: 2 loaves

4 1/2 to 5 cups flour
2 packages yeast
1 tablespoon sugar
2 teaspoons salt
1/4 teaspoon baking soda
2 cups milk
1/2 cup water
cornmeal

1. Combine 3 cups flour*, yeast, sugar, salt and baking soda.
2. Combine liquids and heat to 120 degrees (using a candy thermometer to measure the temperature). Watch for bubbles around the edges. Add to dry mixture and beat well.
3. Stir in enough more flour to make a slightly stiff batter.
4. Spoon batter into two 8 1/2 × 4 1/2-inch pans, that have been greased and sprinkled with cornmeal. Sprinkle cornmeal on top.
5. Let rise 30-40 minutes, covered in a warm place.
6. Microwave each loaf on High 6 1/2 minutes (no longer). Surface will be flat and pale. Let rest 5 minutes before removing from pan.

    *Do not sift flour—fill cup by spooning.

Heavenly Pancakes

As light as a cloud.

Yield: 4-6 pancakes

1 cup sour cream
1 cup cottage cheese
3/4 cup flour
4 eggs, separated
1 tablespoon sugar
1/4 teaspoon salt

1. Mix sour cream and cottage cheese together.
2. Stir in flour and well-beaten egg yolks; beat until smooth.
3. Add salt and sugar; then fold in stiffly beaten egg whites.
4. Cook on hot griddle, greased with butter.

Super Colossal French Toast

Try this easy brunch idea...and pass the butter and maple syrup.

Yield: 4 servings

6 eggs
²/₃ cup orange juice
¹/₃ cup Grand Marnier liqueur
¹/₃ cup milk
3 tablespoons sugar
¹/₄ teaspoon vanilla extract
¹/₄ teaspoon salt
finely grated peel of one orange
8 ³/₄-inch thick slices French bread
butter
powdered sugar
maple syrup

1. Beat eggs in large bowl. Add orange juice, Grand Marnier, milk, sugar, vanilla, salt and peel and mix well.
2. Dip bread into egg mixture, turning to coat all surfaces. Transfer to baking dish in single layer. Pour any remaining egg mixture over top.
3. Cover and refrigerate overnight, turning occasionally.
4. Melt butter in large skillet over medium-high heat. Add bread slices in batches and cook until browned, about 8 minutes. Turn and continue cooking.
5. Arrange on platter and sprinkle with powdered sugar.

Cold-Oven Popovers

Easy to make, a cinch to eat.

Yield: 6 popovers

3 eggs
1 cup milk
1 cup flour
¹/₂ teaspoon salt

1. Grease 6 custard cups heavily.*
2. Beat eggs, milk, flour and salt until smooth.
3. Pour batter into cups, place in a cold oven, turn oven to 450 degrees and bake for 25 minutes from the time the oven is turned on.
4. Pierce with a toothpick to hold for a while without collapsing. Remove from oven.

   *Use plenty of butter to cover custard cups.

Pumpkin Bread

Yield: 1 9 × 9-inch square

4 eggs
1 ¹/₃ cups powdered milk
1 16-ounce can pumpkin
¹/₂ cup plus 2 tablespoons flour
2 tablespoons sugar
1 teaspoon pumpkin pie spice
2 teaspoons vanilla extract
1 teaspoon baking soda

Preheat oven to 350 degrees.
1. Mix all ingredients together and pour into a greased 9 × 9-inch baking pan.
2. Bake at 350 degrees for 30 minutes.

Country Bumpkin Pumpkin Muffins

Yield: 24 muffins

¹/₂ cup butter
1 cup sugar
2 eggs
1 cup cooked and mashed pumpkin
1 cup raisins
3 ¹/₂ cups all-purpose flour
4 teaspoons baking powder
¹/₂ teaspoon ground cinnamon
¹/₂ teaspoon nutmeg
1 teaspoon salt
1 ¹/₄ cups milk

Preheat oven to 400 degrees.
1. Grease muffin tins that are 2 ¹/₂ inches in diameter.
2. Cream the butter and sugar until light and fluffy. Beat in the eggs and pumpkin.
3. Dredge the raisins with ¹/₂ cup of flour. Sift the rest of the flour and the baking powder, cinnamon, nutmeg and salt together.
4. Add the dry ingredients and milk alternately, mixing by hand, just until blended. Do not overmix. Stir in the raisins.
5. Spoon into the prepared muffin tins, filling each cup ³/₄ full.
6. Bake at 400 degrees for 20-25 minutes.

Tea Scones   Microwave

Tea for thee!

Yield: 6-8 scones

2 cups all-purpose flour
pinch of salt
2 teaspoons baking powder
¼ cup butter, cold
2 tablespoons sugar
3 tablespoons currants
1 egg, beaten
4-6 tablespoons milk

1. Sift the flour, salt, and baking powder into a mixing bowl and cut in the butter until mixture resembles bread-crumbs.
2. Add the sugar and currants. Stir in beaten egg and sufficient milk to form a smooth, soft dough.
3. Shape the dough into a ball, then flatten to form a round, about ½-inch thick. Cut into 1½-inch rounds. Place on a piece of non-stick parchment, in the oven, spacing them well apart.
4. Microwave on High for 3 minutes, moving them around.
5. Insert a tester into the center of each scone; if it comes out dry, they are done. If not dry, return for another 30 seconds. Place the scones upside down on a broiler rack. Brown under hot grill, turn over and brown the tops. Serve warm, split and buttered.

Zucchini Bread

Yield: 2 loaves

1 cup vegetable oil
2 1/2 cups sugar
3 eggs
3 cups flour
1/2 teaspoon baking powder
1 teaspoon baking soda
1 teaspoon salt
1 tablespoon ground cinnamon
2 cups grated zucchini
3 tablespoons vanilla extract
1 cup raisins and nuts (optional)

Preheat oven to 350 degrees.
1. Mix oil, sugar and eggs together.
2. Sift flour, baking powder, soda, salt and cinnamon. Add zucchini and vanilla. Blend well.
3. Stir in 1 cup raisins and nuts, if desired.
4. Grease well 2 9 × 5-inch loaf pans and bake at 350 degrees for about 1 hour. Serve plain or with cream cheese.

Waffles Gone Bananas   Low Fat

A treat to serve at breakfast or lunch.

Yield: 6 waffles (90 calories each)

1 package active dry yeast
1 cup non-fat milk, heated to lukewarm
2 eggs, or ¹/₂ cup liquid egg substitute
3 large ripe bananas
2 teaspoons corn oil
2 teaspoons vanilla extract
2 cups whole wheat flour
¹/₄ teaspoon salt
¹/₂ teaspoon cinnamon

1. Sprinkle the yeast on the milk, stir to dissolve and let stand until bubbly.
2. Combine the eggs, bananas, oil and vanilla and mix well. Stir into the yeast mixture.
3. Combine the flour, salt and cinnamon and mix into the egg-yeast mixture, a little at a time, until well blended.
4. Cover the bowl with a towel and let stand in a warm place for about 1 hour.
5. Bake in a hot oiled or Teflon waffle iron for about 5 minutes, or until iron indicates waffle is done.

Dilled Caviar Puffs, 10   Dilly Beans, 8

Brie with Glazed Almonds, 9

Bouillabaisse, 33

Everything But the Kitchen Sink Pasta, 86

Chili con Carne, 98

Oriental Chicken, 156

Baked Corn on the Cob, 174

Fresh Strawberry Souffle, 231

Fruit Daiquiri, 281

White Sangria, 259   19th Hole Frozen Margarita, 258

Eggs, Cheese and Pastas

Blintz Soufflé

Yield: 4 servings

1 package of 8 frozen cheese blintzes, thawed
¹/₂ cup butter, melted
2 cups sour cream
6 eggs, beaten
¹/₄ cup orange juice
¹/₄ cup sugar
2 teaspoons vanilla extract
2 teaspoons salt
sour cream and/or strawberries or blueberries

Preheat oven to 350 degrees.
1. Place blintzes in 2-quart casserole and cover with melted butter.
2. Combine sour cream, eggs, orange juice, sugar, vanilla and salt and pour over blintzes.
3. Bake 1 hour or until puffed and browned.
4. Serve with additional sour cream and pass the berries.

Carmel Omelette   Janet Coles

Never rush a Carmel Omelette! Janet should know—born and bred in Carmel, California, she plays out of the Carmel Valley Ranch. She is an up-and-coming competitor, a real pro in blending flavors as well as burning up a golf course. Janet graduated in 1976 from UCLA with a BS in Kinesiology.

Yield: 2-4 servings

5-6 eggs
2-3 tablespoons water
1½ teaspoons Worcestershire sauce
dash garlic salt
1 teaspoon lemon pepper seasoning
4 ounces Swiss cheese, grated
4 ounces Monterey Jack cheese, grated
6 marinated artichoke hearts, halved
thinly sliced tomato

1. Put eggs, water, Worcestershire sauce and garlic salt into blender. Blend together until fluffy.
2. Pour into large omelette pan, slightly buttered.
3. Sprinkle lemon pepper on top of eggs and cook on low to medium heat. Cover to cook eggs evenly.
4. When the eggs just start to become cooked on top, spread the cheeses over half the omelette; cover and cook on low heat until eggs just begin to get firm.
5. When the cheese starts to melt, put the artichoke hearts and tomatoes on top of cheese.
6. Flip the part without cheese over onto the part with cheese; put cover on and continue to cook. This should take about 5-7 minutes.
   Note: The idea is to cook the eggs evenly plus melt the cheese.

Humpty-Dumpty Eggs

Steve Menchinella

Steve is the golf professional at Sunnyside Country Club, Fresno, California. This delightful and festive combination of flavors will help keep your sunny side up!

Yield: 6 servings

1 tablespoon oil
1 onion, chopped
1 green bell pepper, chopped, without seeds
2 cloves garlic, pressed
**1 28-ounce can peeled tomatoes, chopped, with the
    juice**
3 green chilies, chopped, without seeds
1 teaspoon salt
¹⁄₃ teaspoon freshly ground pepper
1 teaspoon chili powder
1 teaspoon oregano
¹⁄₂ teaspoon ground cumin
6 eggs at room temperature
1 ¹⁄₂ cups grated Monterey Jack cheese
6 corn tortillas, hot

1. Put oil, onion, green pepper and garlic in microwave or in skillet and cook until onion is tender.
2. Add all other ingredients except the eggs, cheese and tortillas and cook until just beginning to boil.
3. Carefully place the eggs on top of the sauce, making a little depression for each egg. Sprinkle the cheese over the entire top.
4. Cover and cook until the eggs are done and the cheese is melted.
5. Serve each egg on a hot tortilla. Spoon remaining sauce over the top of each serving.

There is no difference between a brown or a white egg! Buy which ever is cheaper.

Lox and Cream Cheese Omelette

Unique.

Yield: 2 servings

2 ounces butter or margarine
4 eggs, well beaten
pinch of salt
¼ cup toasted bread (cut in 1-inch cubes)
2 green onions, chopped
approximately ½ cup lox and ½ cup cream cheese,
  mixed
¼ cup fresh parsley, chopped

Preheat oven to 400 degrees.
1. In a large skillet, melt butter until bubbling.
2. Pour in eggs and salt.
3. Add toasted bread chunks and green onions.
4. Continue to cook eggs, lifting the bottom, making sure not to burn them. Once they are no longer runny, let bottom cook for one minute until golden.
5. Spread lox and cream cheese around omelette in dollops. Top with fresh parsley.
6. Place in oven for 3-5 minutes or until cream cheese begins to melt as the eggs rise. Remove and fold one side over to form omelette.

Puffy Omelette   Microwave

Yield: 2 servings

1 tablespoon butter
3 eggs, separated
3 tablespoons milk
¼ teaspoon salt
¼ teaspoon black pepper

1. Put butter in 9-inch round pie plate in microwave oven on High for 30 seconds until melted.
2. Beat the egg whites until stiff peaks form.
3. In separate bowl, whisk the egg yolks, milk, salt and pepper together. Fold the whisked egg whites into the egg yolk mixture. Turn into the pie plate and microwave on Low for 5-6 minutes until the middle of the omelette has just set.
4. Remove from oven, let it stand for 15 seconds, then fold in half, using a palette knife, and turn out on a serving dish.

Options: Sprinkle grated cheese, chopped cooked ham, finely chopped green pepper, diced bacon over the omelette before folding.

Venturi's Special Frittata

Ken Venturi

Born in California, Ken now lives in Florida and is best known as a teacher and commentator for golf telecasts. Among his victories is the United States Open in 1964. This is Ken's version of a frittata.

Yield: 6 servings

2 tablespoons olive oil
2 tablespoons butter or margarine
2 pounds lean ground beef
1 medium onion, finely chopped
1 small clove garlic, finely crushed
2 10-ounce packages frozen spinach, thawed and drained
1/2 teaspoon basil
1/4 teaspoon marjoram
1 teaspoon salt
black pepper to taste
4 eggs

1. Heat oil and butter in large skillet (iron, if you have one) over low heat.
2. Cook meat until brown, stirring to break it up as much as possible.
3. Add the onion and cook about 5 minutes (no need to brown).
4. Add all other ingredients, except the eggs.
5. Now, beat the eggs and stir into skillet over other ingredients and cook just until eggs are done the way you like them.

Chili-Cheese Casserole

High spirited!!

Yield: 8-10 servings

2 4-ounce cans green chilies, drained and seeds removed
1 pound Monterey Jack cheese, coarsely grated
1 pound Cheddar cheese, coarsely grated
4 eggs, separated
²/₃ cup evaporated milk, undiluted
1 tablespoon flour
½ teaspoon salt
⅛ teaspoon pepper
2 medium tomatoes, sliced or 1 15-ounce can tomatoes, drained and sliced

Preheat oven to 325 degrees.
1. Dice chilies.
2. In a large bowl, combine the grated cheese and chilies. Turn into a well-buttered 12 × 8 × 2-inch casserole.
3. In a large bowl, using electric mixer at high speed, beat egg whites just until stiff (peaks form when beater is slowly raised).
4. In a small bowl, combine egg yolks, milk, flour, salt and pepper and mix until well blended.
5. Using a rubber scraper, gently fold beaten egg whites into egg yolk mixture. Spread onto cheese mixture in casserole. Use a fork to "ooze" it through the cheese. Bake for 30 minutes.
6. Remove from oven and arrange sliced tomatoes overlapping around the edge of casserole.
7. Bake 30 minutes longer or until a knife inserted comes out clean.

 If desired, garnish with a sprinkling of chopped green chilies.

Chili Rellenos Casserole
Tom Weiskopf

An Ohio State University graduate, Tom now lives in Arizona with his wife, Jeanne, and their two children. A Million Dollar Winner, he has been named Player-of-the-Year by several groups.

Yield: 6-8 servings

½ cup butter or margarine
1 7-ounce can green chilies (or more to taste)
1 pound Cheddar or Monterey Jack cheese, shredded
3 eggs
¾ teaspoon salt
2 cups milk
1 cup biscuit mix

Preheat oven to 350 degrees.
1. Melt butter in 13 × 9-inch baking dish.
2. Arrange chilies in a layer over bottom of dish. Cover with cheese.
3. Blend eggs, salt, milk and biscuit mix; pour over cheese.
4. Bake at 350 degrees for 35-40 minutes or until golden brown. Have a dish of salsa available for topping.

 If you like keeping your cheese in good shape, wrap it lightly in a cloth wrung out in vinegar water before refrigerating it.

Ham and Cheese Strata

Microwave

You're a winner with this.

Yield: 6 open-faced sandwiches

6 slices firm white bread
1 4½-ounce can deviled ham
6 slices Monterey Jack cheese
1½ cups warm milk
1 tablespoon minced onion
1 tablespoon Worcestershire sauce
½ teaspoon salt
⅛ teaspoon pepper
dash cayenne
3 eggs, beaten

1. Spread bread with deviled ham. Top with cheese slices. Arrange bread in a 2-quart casserole, layering if desired.
2. Mix milk with onions and seasonings. Slowly add to beaten eggs. Stir well. Pour over bread slices; let stand 10 minutes.
3. Microwave on Medium, covered, for 15 minutes, rotating dish once. Let stand, covered, for 5 minutes before serving.

Springtime Ribbon Loaf

Pretty as a picture. Serve it at your next luncheon buffet.

Yield: 1 loaf

2 unsliced loaves of bread
5 8-ounce packages cream cheese, softened
2-3 tablespoons crème de cacao
½ cup raisins
½ cup chopped walnuts
½ cup Leroux Fraise de Bois
½ pint fresh strawberries, hulled and sliced
2-3 tablespoons green crème de menthe
1 bunch watercress, washed and dried

1. Cut crusts off bread and slice the loaves lengthwise into 4 layers. Place bottom layers end to end on a serving platter.
2. Beat one package cream cheese with enough crème de cacao to make it soft and spreadable. Stir in raisins and nuts. Spread on bottom bread layer.
3. Add next layer of bread and press down lightly. Beat 3 packages cream cheese with Fraise de Bois. Spread bread layer with ½ this mixture. Arrange sliced strawberries on top, reserving a few for garnish.
4. Top with another ½ cup cream cheese mixture and another layer of bread. Reserve remaining cheese mixture for frosting loaf.
5. Beat remaining package cream cheese with crème de menthe.
6. Remove coarse stems from watercress, chop and fold into cheese-crème de menthe mixture. Spread over bread layer. Top with remaining bread slices and frost top and sides of loaf with reserved cheese–Fraise de Bois mixture.
7. Decorate with reserved strawberries and watercress.

Classic Welsh Rarebit   Microwave

Yield: 6 servings

2 eggs
1 cup beer
1 tablespoon butter or margarine
1 teaspoon dry mustard
1 teaspoon Worcestershire sauce
dash cayenne
1 pound mild Cheddar cheese, shredded
tomato slices
6 slices toast

1. Beat eggs with rotary beater in a 1½-quart glass casserole.
2. Stir in beer, butter, mustard, Worcestershire sauce, and cayenne. Microwave on High, uncovered, for 2 minutes or until warm.
3. Stir in cheese. Microwave on Medium for 6 to 7 minutes or until cheese is melted. Stir every 2 to 3 minutes.
4. When cheese is melted, blend with rotary beater. Arrange tomato slices on toast; top with cheese mixture.

Green Death   Lauri Peterson

"Too much red pepper the first time." Lauri has now perfected this pasta dish and is actively perfecting her game of golf as well.

Yield: 3-4 servings

12 ounces spinach fettuccine noodles (uncooked)
salted water
1/3 pound butter
red pepper to taste (but watch it!!), 1/8 to 1/4 teaspoon
1/2 cup grated Parmesan cheese
12 ounces cooked ham, diced

1. In a large pot, add spinach noodles to 5 quarts boiling water and 1 tablespoon salt. Boil and stir occasionally for 8-12 minutes to desired texture.
2. In a small saucepan, melt butter. Add cheese and stir. Put a dash of red pepper in for flavor.
3. Warm diced ham and add to sauce.
4. Combine noodles and cheese sauce and serve.

Marinara Sauce   Gary Koch

Gary and his family live in Tampa, Florida, where his interests include fishing, reading, and music. His latest victory was the 1983 Doral-Eastern Open. This recipe is an easy, 30-minute sauce for your favorite pasta.

Yield: 6-7 servings

1/4 cup olive oil
4 large cloves garlic, sliced
2 28-ounce cans plum tomatoes (or 4 cups fresh tomatoes)
4 tablespoons tomato paste
1 1/2 teaspoons oregano
1 1/2 teaspoons basil
1/4 cup chopped parsley
1 1/2 to 2 teaspoons salt
pepper to taste

1. In a 3-quart saucepan, heat the oil and cook the garlic for a minute or two, stirring. Do not brown.
2. Stir in tomatoes, breaking them with a wooden spoon.
3. Add remaining ingredients and bring to a boil.
4. Reduce the heat to low and simmer uncovered for 30 minutes.

 Especially delicious served over spinach noodles with grated Romano cheese on top.

Prize-Winning Mexican Manicotti   Microwave

A champion formula.

Yield: 4-6 servings

½ pound lean ground beef
1 cup refried beans
1 teaspoon dried oregano
½ teaspoon dried cumin
1 package taco-seasoning mix
8 manicotti shells
1½ cups water
1 18-ounce can picante or taco sauce
2 cups sour cream
¼ cup finely chopped onion
¼ cup pitted sliced olives
½ pound Monterey Jack cheese, shredded

1. Combine first 4 ingredients, and ½ package of taco sauce. Mix well. Fill uncooked manicotti shells with mixture. Arrange in baking dish.
2. Combine water, picante sauce and balance of taco seasoning mix; pour over manicotti shells. Cover with vented plastic wrap. Microwave on High 10 minutes, giving dish ½ turn once.
3. Turn shells over, and microwave on Medium for 17-19 minutes until pasta is tender, turning once.
4. Combine sour cream, green onions and olives. Spoon down center of manicotti, top with cheese.
5. Microwave uncovered 2-3 minutes till cheese melts.

Everything But the Kitchen Sink Pasta

Your guests will want seconds and thirds! (See photograph)

Yield: 4 servings

1 pound tomato, spinach or egg pasta shells
2 tablespoons butter
1 tablespoon flour
1 ½ cups milk
1 cup Mozzarella cheese, diced
1 cup Ricotta cheese
½ cup thinly sliced scallions
1 teaspoon oregano
1 teaspoon basil
3 cups broccoli flowerettes, steamed for 1 minute
1 cup diced green pepper
2 cups cherry tomatoes, cut in half
¼ cup chopped parsley

1. Cook pasta according to directions.
2. Melt butter over medium heat, add flour and stir with a whisk for 2 minutes.
3. Stir in the milk and cook for 5 minutes.
4. Add the cheese, stirring constantly; add the scallions, oregano and basil and stir constantly over low heat.
5. When cheese sauce becomes smooth, remove from heat.
6. Toss the hot drained pasta with the broccoli, green peppers and tomatoes. Pour the sauce over all and toss again.
7. Sprinkle with parsley and serve at once.

Pasta Primavera   Microwave

Yield: 4 servings

¹/₂ pound spaghetti or linguine
4 cups vegetables (snow peas, broccoli, asparagus,
  mushrooms, zucchini, tomatoes)
1 clove garlic, minced
¹/₄ cup fresh parsley
¹/₃ cup chopped meat (salami, pepperoni, ham,
  prosciutto)
1 teaspoon salt
¹/₄ teaspoon pepper
2 tablespoons butter
¹/₂ cup cream
¹/₃ cup grated Parmesan cheese

1. Heat 2 quarts water in 3-quart casserole, covered, 9
   minutes on High heat.
2. Add pasta and microwave on High 7 minutes. Stir and
   let stand 3 minutes. Drain.
3. Pile vegetables, garlic, parsley, salt, pepper and meat
   into same casserole. Cover. Microwave on High 4
   minutes.
4. Microwave butter and cream 2 minutes in serving dish.
   Mix in cheese, cooked pasta and vegetables.

 Serve with more cheese.

Besto Pesto Pasta

A perfect performance.

Yield: 4 servings

5 tablespoons chopped parsley
1 8-ounce package cream cheese, softened
1/2 clove garlic, chopped
2 tablespoons grated Parmesan cheese
2 tablespoons olive oil
1 tablespoon salt added to water
2 medium potatoes, peeled and sliced to 1/4-inch thicknesses
1 pound medium-sized noodles

1. Mix parsley, cream cheese, garlic and Parmesan cheese to a smooth consistency. Add oil; set aside.
2. Add salt to a large pan of water. Bring to a boil. Add potatoes. When water boils again, add noodles.
3. Cook until tender (al dente). Before taking noodles and potatoes from water, remove 1 cup of boiling water and add to sauce.
4. Drain noodles and potatoes. Place in bowl and mix with sauce.

Serve with grated cheese.

Spaghetti with White Clam Sauce   Allen Miller

Golf stories are always a topic of conversation when Cindy and Allen entertain. Allen has been on the tour since 1971 and Cindy was formerly with the LPGA tour.

Yield: 4 servings

¾ cup olive oil
3 cloves garlic, finely chopped
½ cup shallots, chopped
¾ cup butter
1½ cups clam juice
3 cups minced clams (about 3 4-ounce cans)
1 cup parsley, finely chopped
dash of oregano
1 pound spaghetti, or linguine, uncooked

1. Heat olive oil, add garlic and shallots. Sauté over low heat until lightly colored.
2. Add butter and clam juice and simmer for 5 minutes.
3. Stir in clams*; add parsley and oregano.
4. Cook spaghetti (or linguine—it tastes even better!).

   *Do not let the clams boil once you put them in or they will get tough.

Classic Ligurian Pesto

This pesto is marvelous as a pasta sauce or as a seasoning for vegetable soups.

Yield: 3-4 servings

2 cups tightly packed fresh basil leaves
¼ cup grated Parmesan cheese
2 cloves garlic, halved
1 tablespoon toasted pine nuts
salt and freshly ground pepper
⅔ cup olive oil approximately
3 tablespoons butter

Combine ingredients in food processor or blender, adding enough olive oil to make thick, smooth sauce.

Spaghetti Pie Lonnie Nielsen

Tastes like lasagna, only much easier to prepare. Can be made ahead and refrigerated for several days. Lonnie and his family live in Belle Plaine, Iowa. He was the Iowa State Amateur Champion in 1976.

Yield: 8 servings

7 ounces spaghetti, uncooked
1 3-ounce can grated Parmesan cheese
1 egg, slightly beaten
4 cups shredded Mozzarella cheese
1 pound ground beef
1 onion, finely chopped
1 15-ounce jar spaghetti sauce
1 4-ounce can mushrooms

Preheat oven to 350 degrees.
1. Cook spaghetti and drain.
2. Mix Parmesan cheese and egg with cooked spaghetti. Put into a greased 9 × 11-inch pan. Top with 2 cups Mozzarella cheese.
3. Brown hamburger with onion and drain off fat. Add spaghetti sauce and mushrooms to hamburger and onion mixture. Pour over sauce.
4. Top with remaining 2 cups Mozzarella cheese. Bake at 350 degrees for about 30 minutes.

Spinach and Green Noodles

Your guests will turn green… with envy!

Yield: 6-8 servings

1 10¾-ounce can cream of mushroom soup
⅓ cup milk
¼ pound mushrooms, sliced and sautéed
4 ounces blue cheese, crumbled
1 8-ounce package spinach noodles, cooked and
**   drained**
2 10-ounce packages frozen chopped spinach,
**   cooked and drained**

Preheat oven to 350 degrees.
1. In a mixing bowl, combine soup and milk.
2. Add cooked mushrooms, blue cheese, noodles and
   spinach. Mix thoroughly.
3. Pour into a buttered 2-quart casserole.
4. Bake, uncovered, at 350 degrees for 1 hour.

Spinach Frittata   Low Fat

It's terrific!

Yield: 4 servings (105 calories each)

1 teaspoon corn oil
1 teaspoon olive oil
1 tablespoon minced onion
3 eggs, lightly beaten or ³/₄ cup liquid egg substitute
¹/₄ cup grated Parmesan or Romano cheese
¹/₂ teaspoon oregano
dash of freshly ground black pepper
1 cup chopped cooked spinach, well drained

1. Heat the oils in an omelette pan.
2. Add the onion and cook until clear and tender.
3. Combine the eggs with half of the cheese, oregano, pepper and spinach and mix well.
4. Pour the egg mixture into the skillet with the onion and cook over very low heat until the edges are lightly browned.
5. Sprinkle the remaining cheese over the top and place under a broiler until the cheese is lightly browned. To serve, cut into wedges.

Meat

Beer Beef Stew   Martha Nause

From Sheboygan, Wisconsin, comes Martha Nause, who
enjoys cooking, sports and photography as well as working
on her golf game. She suggests you start this stew in the
morning and it will be ready to eat for dinner.

Yield: 2-3 servings

1 pound stew meat, cut into bite-sized pieces
1 teaspoon salt
¹/₂ teaspoon pepper
2 onions, sliced
1 8-ounce can undrained mushrooms
1 12-ounce can beer
1 tablespoon vinegar
2 beef bouillon cubes
2 teaspoons sugar
2 cloves garlic
1 teaspoon thyme
2 bay leaves

Optional Additions:
1 15-ounce can tomatoes
celery, potato, carrots or other favorite vegetables

1. Put beef in a crock pot.
2. Combine rest of ingredients and pour over beef.
3. Cover tightly; cook on low 8-10 hours, then on high 4-5
   hours. Remove bay leaves before serving.

Boeuf en Daube (Beef in Casserole)

Yield: 6 servings

3 pounds chuck or stewing beef cut into 2-inch cubes
1 ½ cups red wine
¼ cup cognac
2 tablespoons peanut oil
½ teaspoon thyme
1 bay leaf
1 large onion, coarsely chopped
2 cloves garlic, crushed
2 cups scraped, thinly sliced carrots
½ cup coarsely chopped celery
salt and pepper to taste
½ pound sliced lean bacon, cut in half
water
flour for dredging
2 ½ cups ripe tomatoes, cored, peeled and chopped
2 cups thinly sliced mushrooms
2 cups beef stock, fresh or canned

1. Place the beef in a large mixing bowl and add the wine, cognac, oil, thyme, bay leaf, onion, garlic, carrots, celery, salt and pepper. Cover and refrigerate 3 hours or longer.
2. Place the bacon in a saucepan and add water barely to cover. Simmer 5 minutes and drain.
3. Line a casserole with 3 or 4 pieces of bacon. Drain the beef and reserve the marinade.
4. Dredge each cube of beef in flour and shake to remove any excess.
5. Arrange a layer of beef, add a layer of the marinated vegetables, ⅓ of the tomatoes and ⅓ of the mushrooms.
6. Continue making layers until the ingredients are used, ending with marinated vegetables and bacon.
7. Sprinkle with more salt and pepper. Add beef broth and marinade to cover. Bring to a boil on top of stove. Place in the oven and bake for 15 minutes. Reduce heat to 300 degrees and continue cooking 3 to 4 hours more.
8. Skim the fat from the surface, discard bay leaf, and serve with rice or noodles.

Butter Crust Beef Pie

Bobby Nichols

Expect Southern hospitality when you mention Bobby Nichols. In spite of serious injuries, Bobby continues a career in golf. A devoted family man, his interests are centered on sports and antique cars.

Yield: 6 servings

2 pounds boneless rump roast, cut into bite-sized pieces
2 ½ teaspoons salt
1 teaspoon black pepper
½ teaspoon garlic powder
⅓ cup chopped onion
½ cup self-rising flour
¼ cup oil
2 ½ cups water (add ½ cup more water, if needed)
1 14-ounce can mixed vegetables
½ 4-ounce can early peas

Crust

1 stick melted butter
1 cup self-rising flour
1 cup buttermilk

1. Combine first 6 ingredients in a large bowl. Mix well.
2. Heat oil in a heavy pot. Add beef mixture and brown about 15 minutes.
3. Add 2 ½ cups water and cook 30-45 minutes until tender.
4. Put in baking dish. Add drained vegetables and early peas. Set aside.
5. Mix butter, flour and buttermilk. Pour on top of meat, covering completely.
6. Bake at 350 degrees for 45 minutes. If top is not brown, put under broiler for a few minutes.

 Always prepare all foods at room temperature. This is most important in cooking meat.

Connecticut Beef Supper
Doug Tewell

Doug's career is an inspiration to all of us. Just a stroke or two away from leaving the tour, he has now become one of the game's better players. He attributes his great improvement to lots of hard work and mental discipline. Pam and Doug and their family reside in Edmond, Oklahoma, and play out of Oak Tree Golf Club. This recipe can be prepared in advance, then baked when needed. Kids love it, too!

Yield: 6-8 servings

2 pounds beef for stew, cut into 1-inch cubes
2 large onions, sliced
2 tablespoons olive oil
1 4½-ounce jar mushrooms
4 medium potatoes, pared, thinly sliced
1 10¾-ounce can cream of mushroom soup
¾ cup milk
¾ cup sour cream
1 teaspoon salt
¼ teaspoon pepper
2 cups Cheddar cheese, shredded
fine dry breadcrumbs

1. Season meat with salt and pepper. Cook and stir meat and onions in oil in large skillet over medium heat until meat is brown and onions are tender. Pour off oil.
2. Drain mushrooms, reserving liquid. Add enough water to mushroom liquid to make 1 cup. Stir mushrooms and liquid into meat and onions. Heat to boiling; reduce heat and cover. Simmer 2 hours.
3. Heat oven to 350 degrees. Pour meat mixture into a 9 × 13-inch baking dish.
4. Arrange potatoes over meat. Mix soup, milk, sour cream, salt and pepper; pour over potatoes; sprinkle with cheese.
5. Bake uncovered 1 hour. Sprinkle with breadcrumbs.
6. Continue baking until potatoes are tender and crumbs are brown, 20-30 minutes longer.

Chili à la Boone   The Pat Boone Family

Pat is a keen golfer and a regular participant at the Crosby Pro-Am golf tournament. A devoted family man, he is now doing TV specials with his wife, Shirley.

Yield: 4-6 servings

2 medium onions, chopped
2 tablespoons Wesson oil
1 pound ground beef
2 15-ounce cans solid-packed tomatoes
2 17-ounce cans red kidney beans
2 8-ounce cans tomato sauce
¼ package uncooked spaghetti
salt
chili powder

1. Cook onions in Wesson oil until tender.
2. Add ground beef to skillet and cook until brown.
3. In a large casserole dish, combine the beef and onions with the tomatoes, beans and tomato sauce.
4. Cook the spaghetti and add it to the above mixture. Season to taste with salt and chili powder.
5. Simmer for 1 hour.

Cheese Sauce for Chili à la Boone

1½ pounds sharp Cheddar cheese, grated
1½ pints sour cream
garlic salt
spring onion, chopped

1. Warm cheese and sour cream over low heat, just enough to melt the cheese.
2. Sprinkle a little garlic salt in this sauce, to taste.
3. Serve as a side dish with chopped spring onion.

 A few drops of oil will keep the water from boiling over when cooking spaghetti or macaroni.

Chili con Carne   Glen Campbell

An avid golfer, Glen would like you to know that this dish was probably invented in Texas where chuckwagon cooks fed it to hungry cowboys. According to Glen, the true and finest flavors of this dish begin after a week in the refrigerator! (See photograph)

Yield: many servings

3 pounds ground chuck
3 onions, chopped
1 bell pepper, chopped
2 cloves garlic, crushed
½ teaspoon oregano
¼ teaspoon cumin seed
2 6-ounce cans tomato paste
1 quart water
salt
black pepper, ground
3 tablespoons chili powder
2 17-ounce cans pinto beans

1. Brown beef in iron kettle; add onion and bell pepper.
2. Add garlic, oregano and cumin seed.
3. Add tomato paste, water, salt and pepper to taste and chili powder.
4. Simmer for 1½ hours.
5. Add pinto beans; simmer 30 minutes more.
6. Let sit 2 hours or one week.

Cook's Chili   John Cook

John is as creative in the kitchen as on the course. He will tell you that hard work pays off and the thrill of victory is very tasty. John won the 1983 Canadian Open. He and his family live in Rancho Mirage, California. This chili is also tasty, easy and quick to fix, allowing plenty of time to relax after golf.

Yield: 6 servings

1 ½ pounds ground round beef
1 package chili-seasoning mix
¼ cup chopped onion
1 17-ounce can dark red kidney beans
1 15-ounce can tomato sauce
½ cup water

Spices: thyme, oregano, marjoram leaves (crushed), basil leaves (crushed). Use spices to suit your own taste.

1. Brown the meat; drain grease.
2. Add package of chili seasoning mix and stir for a few minutes, until well blended.
3. Add onions; stir for a couple of minutes, until blended.
4. Add rest of ingredients, stir and simmer for at least 45 minutes—the longer the better!

Sourdough or garlic bread is good to dip in chili.

Raymond's Spicy Chili
Ray Floyd

Raymond Floyd has been a professional since 1961 and each year his game gets better. He has won staggering amounts of money in events all over the world. When he is at home in Miami Beach, Florida, he loves this chili, which he prepares.

Yield: 6 servings

3 pounds lean beef
¼ cup oil
2 cloves garlic, finely chopped
1 small onion, finely chopped
1 ½ cups tomato sauce
1 10-ounce can beer
3 tablespoons chili powder
¾ teaspoon ground cumin
1 teaspoon paprika
1 teaspoon salt
¼ teaspoon black pepper
¼ teaspoon cayenne pepper

1. Have butcher cut the meat in cubes the size of the tip of your thumb. In a heavy pot, heat the oil. Put in the meat and cook over low heat until the meat turns grey. *Do not let it brown.*
2. Add the garlic and onions, cover and simmer for about 8 minutes.
3. Add the tomato sauce and beer, cover and let it simmer for about 12 minutes.*
4. Mix all the remaining ingredients and add them to the meat.
5. Cover and cook for 1½ to 2 hours over low heat. The meat is done when it breaks apart with a fork.

   *If the consistency is too thin, thicken it as follows: Mix 2 tablespoons of flour and water into a thin paste, add to the chili and cook for 10 minutes.

 The chili is better the next day and freezes well.

Chuck Roast   Marlene Floyd DeArmar

As a stewardess for United Airlines, Marlene spent much of her free time playing golf in amateur tournaments. She later joined the LPGA tour in 1976. From a golfing family, she also enjoys tennis, skiing, and home decorating.

Yield: 4 servings

2 to 2¼-pound chuck roast
2 bouillon cubes
3½ cups water
¾ teaspoon garlic salt
½ teaspoon pepper

Preheat oven to 375 degrees.
1. In a covered casserole dish, combine beef, bouillon cubes, water and seasonings.
2. Bake at 375 degrees for 1½ hours or 20 minutes per pound.

Inexpensive and delicious! Serve with:

Baked Potatoes

1. Drizzle Wesson oil over peeled, cubed potatoes.
2. Sprinkle salt over potatoes to coat.
3. Bake in a 375-degree oven, uncovered, about one hour or until done.

Enchiladas Texas Style Brad Bryant

Brad is a Texan now living in Florida. He and his wife, Sue, enjoy entertaining in the Texas style and often serve enchiladas, refried beans and tacos.

Yield: 6 servings

Enchilada Sauce Mix (Make Ahead):

1 cup flour
½ cup cornstarch
½ cup ground red chili powder
1 teaspoon garlic powder
1 teaspoon oregano
½ teaspoon black pepper
1 teaspoon salt
2 tablespoons paprika
1 teaspoon red pepper
1 teaspoon cumin

Mix all ingredients well. This makes 2 cups.

Enchiladas

½ cup of above sauce mix
4 cups water
2 pounds ground beef
1 medium onion, chopped
12 ounces Cheddar cheese, grated
12 corn tortillas, softened*
shredded lettuce
chopped tomato

1. Mix together sauce mixture and water.
2. Brown meat and onion and drain off fat. Add sauce and heat through.
3. For each serving, layer 1 tortilla, some meat sauce and some cheese. Repeat so each serving is a double-decker. Top with shredded lettuce and chopped tomato.

   *To soften tortillas, put one at a time in hot oil for a few seconds. Do not leave in hot oil too long or they will get too crisp.

Green Enchilada Casserole

Jacky Cupit

The 1961 Canadian Open winner, Jacky now resides in Dallas, Texas. Try this once and you will want to do it again.

Yield: 6-8 servings

2 pounds ground beef
1 cup diced onion
1 teaspoon paprika
1 teaspoon cumin
salt to taste
fried tortillas
1 4-ounce can chopped mushrooms
1 3-ounce can jalapeño peppers
1 4-ounce can whole green chilies
2 10¾-ounce cans cream of mushroom soup
¾-1 pound cheese, grated

1. Fry hamburger and onion together; sprinkle with paprika, cumin, and salt while meat is browning.
2. Line casserole with soft tortillas (sides and bottom).
3. Spread hamburger mixture on the tortillas; sprinkle chopped mushrooms, jalapeños, and whole green chilies over top of hamburger.
4. Pour soup over top. Cover with soft tortillas.
5. Top with grated cheese and bake until cheese melts.

BBQ Blue Cheese Flank Steak

Roger Maltbie

A consistent winner, Roger was born in Modesto, California and turned professional in 1973. When off the tour, Roger loves to cook his favorite specialty. The blue cheese taste is not too strong; even though Roger's wife, Donna, does not care for blue cheese, she loves this dish! Try it with home fries, a green salad and a glass of red wine.

Yield: 4-6 servings

1 large flank steak, approximately 2 pounds, pounded just once
small amount cooking oil
3 ounces blue cheese
rosemary leaves, crushed

1. Rub cooking oil lightly on both sides of steak.
2. Spread crumbled blue cheese on steak, then roll and tie.
3. Roll steak in the crushed rosemary leaves.
4. Barbecue 20-25 minutes for medium-rare steak.

Marinated Flank Steak

Bob Eastwood

Bob lives in Stockton, California, and plays out of Dry Creek Ranch Golf Club, built by his family. This is always a winning recipe. Bob enjoys it best barbecued on the patio.

Yield: 4-6 servings

1 8-ounce bottle Italian salad dressing
1 onion, cut in rings and separated
1 6-ounce can tomato sauce
2 tablespoons Worcestershire sauce
½ cup brown sugar
1 tablespoon lemon juice
large flank steak, about 2 pounds

1. Cook onion in salad dressing until onion is clear; do not boil.
2. Add all ingredients, except steak and simmer a few minutes. Cool sauce completely.
3. Cut flank steak into strips approximately ½-inch thick. Cut diagonally, on the bias.
4. Cover with above marinade and allow to marinate at least 8 hours, out of refrigerator, or overnight in refrigerator.*
5. Barbecue approximately 5 minutes on each side, depending on heat of fire.

Save the marinade…it's great on chicken, ribs, etc.

*The longer the meat marinates, the better it tastes.

Stuffed Frankfurters Microwave

Yield: 6 servings

1 pound large frankfurters (6-8)
½ cup water
¼ cup butter or margarine, melted
2 cups corn-bread stuffing mix
1 beaten egg
2 tablespoons sliced green onions
½ cup shredded Cheddar cheese

1. Cut frankfurters lengthwise, not all the way through. Place in a shallow baking dish.
2. In a mixing bowl, stir together remaining ingredients, except cheese. Mound mixture in cut franks.
3. Microwave on High for 4-8 minutes or until heated through.
4. Sprinkle cheese on top and microwave 1-2 minutes, until cheese is melted.

Oreo Hamburgers   Toney Penna

Toney Penna designs hamburgers as creatively as he designs golf clubs. Each one is a masterpiece. Toney now lives in Jupiter, Florida.

Yield: 4 servings

**1 pound chopped sirloin, hamburger or ground
    round
2 ounces blue cheese
mustard
a little olive oil**

1. With half the meat, make one fairly thick meat patty.*
2. In a small deep dish, mix the blue cheese with the mustard and olive oil.
3. Put a small 1/4-inch cheese patty in the center of prepared thick sirloin patty and cover that with another patty of meat. Pinch sides together.
4. Cook on grill according to taste.

   *Use wet hands when forming patty.

Sweet-Sour Meatballs   Microwave

A real crowd pleaser.

Yield: About 3 cups

**1 10³/₄-ounce can condensed tomato soup
3 tablespoons lemon juice
1/4 cup packed brown sugar
3/4 teaspoon seasoned salt
1 pound ground beef
1 onion, finely chopped
1 teaspoon salt
1 13¹/₄-ounce can pineapple chunks, drained**

1. Combine soup, lemon juice, brown sugar and salt in an 8 × 8 × 2-inch glass dish. Microwave on High for 7 minutes, stirring twice.
2. Combine ground beef, onion, and salt.
3. Roll ground beef into small meatballs. Place meatballs in sauce. Spoon some sauce over meatballs.
4. Microwave on Medium for 10 minutes. Turn halfway through. Stir in pineapple. Microwave on High for 1 minute.

Charley's Pride   Charley Pride

Also known as Hamburgers!! A new twist on a recipe for hamburger. Charley suggests you can broil, fry or barbecue them and top them with anything that pleases you. Charley, a popular singer, sponsors the Golf Fiesta played at the University of Mexico.

Yield: 4 servings

1 pound ground beef
1 medium onion, grated
1 medium potato, grated
1 egg, beaten
salt and pepper

1. Mix together ground beef, grated onion and grated potato.
2. Add beaten egg, salt and pepper. Make into patties.

Serve on buns.
Lettuce and tomato optional.

Easy Meatloaf   Patty Berg

Patty Berg remains one of the most important ambassadors of women's golf, with numerous honors and achievements bestowed upon her throughout the years. She especially likes to make this easy meatloaf ahead of time and serve it cold for sandwiches.

Yield: 6 servings

1 ½ pounds lean ground beef
½ cup catsup
2 eggs
1 medium onion, chopped
2 slices bread, rinsed with cold water and squeezed
     dry
1 teaspoon Worcestershire sauce
½ teaspoon salt
¼ teaspoon pepper
⅓ cup milk

Preheat oven to 325 degrees.
1. Combine all the ingredients into bowl; mix well.
2. Shape into a loaf and place in a loaf pan.
3. Spread more catsup on the top.
4. Bake at 325 degrees for approximately 1 ½ hours.

Italian Stuffed Meatloaf
George Burns III

Always looking for a new way to fix meatloaf? Here's an interesting recipe Irene and George Burns know you will love. The leftovers make great sandwiches, too. George won the 39th Crosby National Pro-Am tournament in 1980, nudging out Dan Pohl by one stroke.

Yield: 6 servings

2 pounds chopped chuck beef
1 raw egg
1/2 cup Italian-seasoned breadcrumbs
1/4 cup grated Parmesan cheese
1 hard-cooked egg, sliced
1 8-ounce package Mozzarella cheese, sliced into 8 pieces
4 slices ham

Preheat oven to 350 degrees.
1. In large bowl, mix meat, egg, breadcrumbs and grated cheese. When well blended, put meat onto large sheet of wax paper. Pat into large round pancake, approximately 1/2-inch thick.
2. Down center of pancake, in a line, place egg slices on top of Mozzarella cheese slices, and add ham on top of egg. End with remaining cheese.
3. Fold meat over and press with fingers to seal.
4. Shape to form large sausage. Using wax paper, roll loaf into baking pan.*
5. Bake at 350 degrees for 40 minutes. Remove from oven and let set for 10 minutes. Slice and serve.

   *May be prepared one day ahead and refrigerated.

 Meat is easier to work with if left out about one hour before preparing.

Mexicale Beef   Jim Langley

Jim is the golf professional at Cypress Point Country Club,
Pebble Beach. He and his wife Louella often take this dish
to the pot-luck dinners they attend with their family.
Mexicale Beef originated with Dave Stockton, winner of
two PGA championships, and his wife, Cathy.

Yield: 6-8 servings

1 pound lean ground beef
1 tablespoon instant minced onion
1/2 teaspoon garlic salt
2 8-ounce cans tomato sauce
1 cup chopped black olives
1/2 pint sour cream
1/2 pint small-curd cottage cheese
3/4 of 1 4-ounce can diced, seedless chilies
1 6 1/2-ounce package tortilla chips
2 cups grated Monterey Jack cheese

Preheat oven to 350 degrees.
1. Fry the beef until the pink disappears and it is crumbly.
   Drain off fat.
2. Add onions, garlic salt, tomato sauce and olives to beef.
3. Combine sour cream, cottage cheese and green chilies.
4. Crush tortilla chips, saving a few for garnish.
5. Layer 1/2 of chips in a well-buttered 2 1/2-quart casserole
   dish, followed by 1/2 beef and 1/2 sour-cream mixture.
6. Sprinkle 1/2 the cheese on top and repeat procedure.
7. Bake uncovered at 350 degrees 30-35 minutes or until
   bubbly. Garnish with reserved chips.

Grandma's Winter Stew
Chris Roderick

This stew is certainly a meal in itself. What could be better or more complete? Serve it in a soup tureen with lots of crusty bread. Chris is the golf professional at the Olympic Club, San Francisco, California.

Yield: 6-8 servings

2 pounds beef chuck, cut in 1½-inch cubes
4 tablespoons all-purpose flour
4 tablespoons salad oil
1 10¾-ounce can beef consommé
1 large onion, chopped (about 1½ cups)
1 clove garlic, minced
1½ cans (28 ounces each) whole tomatoes, cut up, with juice
1½ teaspoons salt
¼ teaspoon pepper
¼ teaspoon sugar
1 teaspoon basil
1 teaspoon rosemary, crushed
½ teaspoon oregano
3 large potatoes, pared and cut into chunks
4 carrots, pared and sliced ¼-inch thick
4 ribs celery, sliced on bias
1 16-ounce can green beans, drained
2 cups sliced mushrooms

Preheat oven to 350 degrees.
1. Dust chunks of beef with flour (a plastic bag is good).
2. Using a large heavy kettle, brown meat in hot oil.
3. Add consommé, stirring to mix in all browned bits. Add onion and garlic, tomatoes, salt and pepper, sugar, basil, rosemary, and oregano.
4. Cover and cook in preheated 350-degree oven for 1 to 1½ hours.
5. Add potatoes, carrots and celery and return to oven to continue cooking, covered, for 1 hour longer.
6. Add beans and mushrooms. Return to oven and cook 30 minutes longer or until meat and vegetables are tender.

Mulligan Stew   Doug Tewell

You will want seconds of this dish. "This is a very easy
version of a great Southern favorite we got at this year's
Southern Open from a Georgia friend," says Pam, Doug's
wife.

Yield: 6 servings

2 pounds ground beef
1 10-ounce package frozen chopped onions
3 10-ounce cans Castleberry BBQ Pork
4 5-ounce cans Swanson White Chicken Meat
1 32-ounce bottle catsup
1 12-ounce can whole corn
1 teaspoon lemon-pepper seasoning
1 teaspoon seasoned salt
1 teaspoon onion salt
¼ cup sugar

1. Brown together the ground beef and onions.
2. Add all other ingredients; mix well and cook about 2
   hours.

Rhodesian Bumba Zinkey Shepherd's Pie   Nick Price

Nicholas Raymond Leige Price is a name to reckon with. From South Africa, he won the World Series of Golf the first time he saw the Firestone Country Club. That victory was worth $100,000 and a ten-year exemption. This typical Rhodesian dish makes a filling meal for four.

Yield: 4 servings

4 large potatoes
1/2 cup milk
butter
1 1/2 pounds lean ground sirloin*
1 15-ounce can peeled tomatoes
1 onion, chopped
meat seasoning (Accent)
salt and pepper
selections of powdered herbs
2 tablespoons tomato catsup
wine glass of red wine
grated cheese
butter to dot on top

1. Boil potatoes, mash well with a little milk and butter. Put potatoes aside.
2. Put meat in a saucepan and add tomatoes, onion, meat seasoning, salt and pepper, powdered herbs of your choice, tomato catsup and wine.
3. Bring to a boil and simmer for 30 minutes.
4. Place meat in a baking dish. Make sure consistency is thickish; thicken either by boiling off excess liquid or adding a little cornstarch.
5. Spread mashed potatoes evenly on top of meat; sprinkle with grated cheese and dot with butter.
6. Brown under broiler.

*Use top-grade lean sirloin.

Tangy Tortilla Casserole
Gene Littler

Gene and his wife, Shirley, enjoy California-style living
and often serve Mexican food when they entertain. This
casserole has a zesty taste and is always a family favorite.
Gene, a professional since 1954, has undergone major
surgery and still maintains an exempt status. He joined the
senior tour in 1981.

Yield: 8-10 servings

1 ½ pounds ground beef
1 medium onion, chopped
1 16-ounce can tomatoes
1 10-ounce can enchilada sauce
½ of 1 10-ounce can sliced olives with liquid
1 teaspoon salt
¼ teaspoon garlic powder
⅛ teaspoon pepper
¼ cup salad oil
8 corn tortillas, halved
1 egg
1 cup small-curd cottage cheese
½ pound Monterey Jack cheese, sliced thinly
½ cup shredded Cheddar cheese
1 large package tortilla chips, crushed

Preheat oven to 350 degrees.
1. Brown beef and onion in a large frying pan. Blend in
   tomatoes, enchilada sauce, olives with liquid, salt, garlic
   powder, and pepper.
2. Bring mixture to a boil; reduce heat and simmer, uncovered, for about 20 minutes, stirring occasionally.
3. Sauté tortillas one at a time in heated oil in a small frying
   pan a few seconds on each side, until softened.

4. Beat egg and mix in cottage cheese.
5. Spread ⅓ of the meat mixture in a greased 9 × 13-inch casserole. Next, spread ½ of the Jack cheese, then ½ of the cottage cheese mixture and ½ of the tortillas. Repeat the layers, ending with remaining ⅓ meat sauce.
6. Top with Cheddar cheese and a border of crushed tortilla chips.
7. Bake uncovered in a 350-degree oven for 20 minutes or until thoroughly heated.
8. Cut into squares or wedges.

Steak Teriyaki   Mark Lye

Mark is a "meat and potato" man and enjoys this dish. It's easy to prepare and delicious with a fine wine after hours on the golf course. Mark has played as an amateur in California, Europe and Australia.

Yield: 4 servings

5-8 ounces Kikkoman Teriyaki Marinade Sauce
1½ to 2-pound Delmonico or rib-eye steak
3 tablespoons cooking oil
3 tablespoons butter
2 medium white onions, sliced in ¼- to ½-inch slices
2 medium bell peppers, sliced in ¼- to ½-inch slices
1 pound mushrooms, sliced

1. Slice steak into 12-inch strips. Place meat in marinating pan and pour on at least 5 ounces teriyaki marinade. Place in refrigerator.
2. Heat together the oil and butter.
3. Add onions and peppers to oil and butter mixture. Stir fry for 3-4 minutes.
4. Add sliced mushrooms. Stir fry for 3-4 minutes longer. Drain moisture from skillet.
5. Add meat and marinade and cook everything together over medium heat until meat is done to personal preference.

Lamb Avgolemono

A tasty egg-lemon sauce which might be slightly difficult to make, only the first time. Use good quality lamb and cut across the grain.

Yield: 6 servings

¼ cup butter plus 1 tablespoon olive oil
2 onions, chopped
2 cloves garlic, minced
3 pounds leg of lamb, cubed
2 tablespoons chopped parsley
¾ cup white wine
2 tablespoons flour
1 teaspoon salt
½ teaspoon pepper
enough water to cover
2 14-ounce cans artichoke hearts in brine, drained and halved

1. Over medium heat melt butter and olive oil. Gently braise onion, garlic and lamb.
2. Cook until all red is gone from meat and approximately half of the moisture has evaporated. Add parsley, wine, and flour (which has been dissolved in 3 tablespoons of water).
3. Add salt, pepper and enough water to cover.
4. Cover and simmer gently for 1 hour.
5. When lamb is almost done, carefully place artichoke hearts on top of meat mixture until heated through.

Egg-Lemon Sauce

3 eggs, separated, at room temperature
juice of 2 or 3 lemons, about ¼ to ½ cup (depending upon the degree of lemon flavor desired.)

1. Beat egg whites until stiff. Add egg yolks and continue beating.
2. Add lemon juice very slowly, beating constantly to keep from curdling.

3. Add 1 cup of stock from meat mixture, beating until well blended.
4. Turn off heat, then return egg mixture to lamb. Let steep for a few minutes and serve immediately with a crusty French bread.

Pomegranate Lamb   Amy Alcott

Amy set the tone for her career when she won the Orange Blossom Classic, only her third event. She has never had a non-winning season. Rich, tangy and colorful are her words to describe this delicious lamb feast.

Yield: 10 servings

1 5- to 6-pound leg of lamb
1 cup unsweetened pomegranate juice
$1/2$ cup dry red wine
2 large onions
1 lemon, unpeeled and chopped
3 cloves garlic
1 teaspoon black pepper
1 tablespoon basil leaves
1 teaspoon salt

Have butcher butterfly the leg of lamb.
1. In blender container, combine pomegranate juice, red wine, onions, lemon, garlic, pepper, basil and salt. Purée. Rub marinade well into lamb.
2. Place meat in shallow glass or enameled pan. Pour remaining marinade over meat. Marinate in refrigerator overnight.
3. Wipe off excess marinade. Cook over medium coals until meat thermometer reaches 145 degrees for medium-rare doneness.
4. Wait 5-10 minutes before carving.

Stuffed Leg of Lamb

Hale Irwin

This recipe is from a good friend, Julie Marsh, wife of Graham Marsh, a professional golfer living in Perth, Australia. It is now a family favorite of the Irwins'.

Yield: 6-8 servings

½ cup long-grain rice
1-2 cups water
3 ounces butter
3 strips bacon, chopped
1 large onion, finely choppped
1 clove garlic, crushed
3 cups fresh white breadcrumbs
3 tablespoons chopped parsley
4 shallots, chopped
½ teaspoon rosemary
¼ teaspoon thyme
salt and pepper
1 egg, slightly beaten
1 3- to 4-pound boned leg of lamb

Preheat oven to 350 degrees.
1. Gradually add rice to boiling salted water. Cook until tender. Drain rice.
2. Heat butter in pan, add bacon, onion, and garlic.
3. Sauté gently until onion is tender.
4. Place rice, breadcrumbs, parsley, shallots, rosemary, thyme, salt and pepper and egg in bowl.
5. Add onion mixture, with butter in pan, and mix thoroughly.
6. Stitch up one end of lamb. Stuff through other end and stitch.
7. Cook about 2 hours at 350 degrees.

 Meats and poultry are best roasted at low temperatures. This cuts down the shrinkage and makes the meat juicier.

Lamb Shanks

Yield: 4 servings

4 meaty lamb shanks
4 cloves garlic, crushed
½ lemon
1 cup flour
2 teaspoons salt
½ teaspoon pepper
½ cup salad oil
1 10-ounce can beef or chicken consommé
1 cup water
½ cup dry vermouth
1 medium onion, chopped
2 bay leaves
4 carrots, sliced
4 stalks celery, sliced

Preheat oven to 350 degrees.
1. Rub lamb with garlic and lemon. Let stand for 10 minutes.
2. Combine flour, salt and pepper in a paper bag; shake shanks to coat. Save the flour.
3. Brown shanks in hot oil; remove from pan.
4. Add 4 tablespoons seasoned flour to the pan drippings, stir with a wire whisk and brown the flour.
5. Add the consommé, water, vermouth; cook until lightly thickened; add onion and bay leaves.
6. Place the shanks in large baking dish; pour sauce over.
7. Refrigerate until ready to bake. Bake at 350 degrees for 1½ hours. Turn and add carrots and celery; bake another hour. Remove bay leaves before serving.

Pork Chops and OJ

Yield: 4 servings

1 large onion, sliced
1 tablespoon butter
1 tablespoon cooking oil
flour
salt and pepper
4 loin pork chops, 1 ½ inches thick
2 cups orange juice
1 ½ tablespoons sugar
2 teaspoons ground ginger

1. Sauté onion slices in butter and oil until transparent; do not brown. Remove from pan. Dredge chops in flour. Season with salt and pepper. Brown chops in remaining butter and oil, about 7 minutes each side.
2. Return onions to pan.
3. Combine orange juice, sugar and ginger.
4. Pour 1 cup over chops and onions. Simmer over low heat for 1 hour 45 minutes, or until very tender, adding more orange juice, if needed.
5. Remove chops to platter and place in warm oven.
6. Add remaining orange juice to pan and boil down to thicken into syrupy consistency. Pour over chops or pass separately.

♀ Wonderful with mashed potatoes and fresh green beans.

Super Spareribs   Microwave

Yield: 3-4 servings

1 side spareribs, separated into ribs
salt and pepper
fine herbs
½ cup flour
1 teaspoon ground ginger
½ cup brown sugar
heavy syrup from a 16-ounce can Bartlett pears

Preheat oven to 350 degrees.
1. Place spareribs in roasting pan. Dust with herbs, salt and pepper.
2. Bake at 350 degrees for 1 hour. Drain off all fat.
3. Sprinkle ribs with flour, ginger and brown sugar.
4. Pour the syrup over and bake about 1½ hours more until very brown, turning and basting several times.

Alternate Method:
Step 2 (above) in microwave oven for 15 minutes on High covered with wax paper. Then proceed to Step 4 (above) and cook in oven for about 45 minutes to 1 hour.

Veal Monterey

Yield: 6 servings

8 thin slices avocado
16 veal slices (about 2 pounds) pounded thin
8 thin slices tomato, drained on paper towels
8 slices Monterey Jack cheese
8 tablespoons grated Parmesan cheese
8 ounces cooked tiny shrimp
salt and pepper
flour
2 eggs, beaten
2 cups breadcrumbs
2-4 tablespoons butter

1. Arrange 1 avocado slice over veal slice. Top with 1 tomato slice and 1 slice Monterey Jack cheese.
2. Sprinkle with 1 tablespoon Parmesan cheese. Season with salt and pepper. Top with 1 ounce shrimp and cover with another veal slice.
3. Pinch edges of veal together tightly to form a package. Repeat with remaining veal. Refrigerate until firm, about 1½ hours.
4. Dust veal with flour. Dip into beaten egg and then roll in breadcrumbs, covering completely.
5. Heat butter in large skillet; add veal in batches (do not crowd) and sauté until lightly browned.

Jane's Vienna Schnitzel Aussie Style Jane Crafter

Jane comes from Down Under: specifically, Perth, Australia, where she was a qualified pharmacist. She decided to join the tour after an impressive amateur resumé. Called "Crafty" by friends, she also enjoys music and reading.

Yield: 4 servings

4 veal cutlets
1 egg
2 cups breadcrumbs
butter
salt and pepper
lemon

1. Tenderize veal cutlets with meat mallet and flatten out to ¼-inch thickness.
2. Beat egg in bowl. Dip each cutlet into egg, then coat with breadcrumbs.
3. Season with salt and pepper. Place in refrigerator.
4. Melt butter in frying pan. Cook cutlets quickly, browning on each side.
5. Ready in approximately 8-10 minutes, depending on thickness.

 Serve garnished with lemon.

Venison Roast   J. C. Snead

J. C. Snead is one of the game's more colorful personalities, known for his sense of humor. A few years ago, J. C. decided to go by his full name, Jesse Carlyle. After a few weeks of not playing well, he informed everyone he was going back to using J. C. because "Jesse Carlyle hasn't been playing worth a damn!"

Yield: 4-6 servings

1 venison loin sliced in ½- to ¾-inch thick slices
1 stick butter
3 to 4 cloves garlic, crushed
salt and pepper to taste

1. Pound the venison slices to tenderize.
2. Melt butter with crushed garlic cloves.
3. Baste venison slices with garlic butter. Salt and pepper to taste.
4. Grill for 7 to 12 minutes until medium rare. Do not overcook. Look for "pink center".

Veal Scaloppine   Low Fat

For lovers of good food.

Yield: 4 servings (190 calories each)

8 slices veal scaloppine, about 1 pound
1 tablespoon prepared mustard
2 teaspoons mustard seed
2 tablespoons unsalted margarine
¼ cup water

1. Put each slice of veal between sheets of plastic wrap and pound lightly.
2. Brush both sides of the meat with the mustard. Sprinkle with mustard seeds.
3. Heat the margarine in a skillet and add the scaloppine. Cook for about one minute over high heat. Turn and cook the other side. Transfer to a warm platter.
4. Add the water to the skillet. When it boils rapidly, pour and scrape the pan sauce over the veal.

♀   Serve with hot, fresh tomato sauce.

○○○○○○○○○○○○○○○○○○○○○

Fish and Seafood

○○○○○○○○○○○○○○○○○○○○○

South Texas Fried Bass   Ed Fiori

When Ed is off the tour and back home in Stafford, Texas, he always manages to do some fishing. You should enjoy his recipe for fried bass.

Yield: 2-20 servings

5 or 6 fresh bass—more people, more fish
yellow cornmeal
cayenne pepper
salt and black pepper
peanut oil

1. Fillet bass. Cut into 2-inch pieces. Chill in ice water.
2. In a large grocery bag, mix cornmeal, cayenne pepper, salt and pepper.
3. In a 4-quart deep fryer, heat peanut oil to 375 degrees. Put kitchen match to hot oil; match will light at 375 degrees.
4. Take 5 or 6 fillets, drop in bag, shake well. Remove and cook in oil.

  Fish will float when done.

Cheese-Sauced Halibut

Yield: 6 servings

2 pounds halibut
¼ cup margarine or butter
¼ cup flour
¼ teaspoon garlic salt
dash of pepper
1 ½ cups milk
½ cup dry white wine
3 tablespoons grated Parmesan cheese
dash of paprika

Preheat oven to 350 degrees.
1. Place fish in greased baking dish.
2. In saucepan, melt margarine; blend in flour, garlic salt, pepper; add milk and wine. Cook and stir until thick and bubbly.
3. Stir in 1 tablespoon cheese. Pour sauce over fish.
4. Bake at 350 degrees for 20-25 minutes.
5. Sprinkle remaining cheese and paprika over top; put under broiler for 1 more minute.

Baked Salmon with Mustard Sauce

Yield: 4 servings

1 cleaned whole or half salmon
salt
melted butter or margarine
parsley
lemon wedges

Preheat oven to 400 degrees.
1. Clean and dry salmon; sprinkle with salt inside and out.
2. Place in well-greased baking dish; brush well with butter.
3. Bake in a 400-degree oven about 10 minutes per pound. Garnish with parsley and lemon wedges. Serve with Mustard Sauce (below).

Mustard Sauce with Grapes

1 ½ cups Tokay grapes
1 tablespoon sugar
1 tablespoon minced onion
2 tablespoons oil
¾ cup tarragon vinegar
2 tablespoons prepared mustard
dash salt

1. Halve and seed grapes. Mix remaining ingredients in saucepan and heat to boiling, but do not boil.
2. Stir in grapes; serve at once with baked salmon.

Cold Poached Salmon Microwave

A "fair way" to end the day.

Yield: 3-4 servings

1 pound fresh salmon
1 ¼ cups water
2 tablespoons red or white wine
1 small onion, quartered
¼ teaspoon black pepper
1 teaspoon salt
6 peppercorns, crushed
1 bay leaf
pinch of dried dill, tarragon, or dried mixed herbs
¼ cucumber, peeled and thinly sliced, for garnish
mayonnaise or tartar sauce

1. Lay the salmon, cut side up, in a dish which it fits snugly. Combine the water, wine, onion, seasoning and herbs. Pour over the fish. Cover and microwave on Medium for 6-8 minutes.
2. Turn the salmon over half-way through cooking. Leave the fish to cool in the liquid.
3. Remove the skin from the salmon. Carefully transfer the fish to a serving dish. Garnish with the cucumber slices and serve with mayonnaise or tartar sauce.

Salmon Cheese Pie

Yield: 6 servings

pastry for one 9-inch pie
1 16-ounce can salmon
1 cup shredded Cheddar cheese
¾ cup sliced mushrooms
½ cup pitted and sliced olives
2 tablespoons chopped parsley
3 eggs
¼ teaspoon dry mustard
¼ teaspoon salt
⅛ teaspoon pepper
1 cup milk
⅓ cup cream or evaporated milk

Preheat oven to 425 degrees.
1. Line a pie plate with pastry.
2. Drain and pick out the bones of the salmon, reserving the liquid. Flake the salmon and spread in pie shell.
3. Sprinkle with cheese, mushrooms, olives and parsley.
4. Combine eggs, mustard, salt and pepper, milk, cream and salmon liquid. Pour carefully over salmon mixture.
5. Bake at 425 degrees for 10 minutes; reduce heat to 350 degrees and bake 30 minutes or longer until filling is set.
6. Remove from oven, let stand 10 minutes; cut into wedges.

 A shopping tip... old eggs are smooth and shiny. Fresh eggs look rough and chalky.

Sole in Tomato and Mushroom Sauce   Microwave

Exceptional execution.

Yield: 4 servings

1 small bunch scallions, trimmed and thinly sliced
2 tablespoons butter or margarine
2 cups sliced mushrooms
1 pound tomatoes, skinned and quartered
1 tablespoon chopped parsley
2 tablespoons basil
¼ teaspoon sugar
½ teaspoon salt
¼ teaspoon black pepper
4 pieces Dover sole, skinned and trimmed

1. To prepare the sauce, combine the scallions and butter in a large shallow dish. Microwave on High for 3 minutes, stirring once during cooking.
2. Add the mushrooms and microwave on High for 3 minutes. Stir in the remaining ingredients, except the fish, cover loosely with plastic wrap and microwave on Low for 15 minutes. Let stand while cooking the fish.
3. Place the fish in a suitable glass pan. Season with salt and pepper and cover with plastic wrap. Microwave on High for 12-15 minutes, or until fish easily flakes.
4. Meanwhile, break up the vegetables in the sauce, with a potato masher. Spoon the sauce on top of the fish before serving.

Petrale Sole Duxelles

A European delight.

Yield: 6 servings

1 tablespoon olive oil
1 tablespoon flour
1/4 pound mushrooms, chopped
1/3 cup chopped shallots
3/4 teaspoon tarragon
1/2 cup chopped parsley
1/3 cup dry white wine
1/4 cup whipping cream
2 pounds Petrale sole
1/8 teaspoon salt
1/8 teaspoon pepper
1/8 teaspoon paprika
3 slices firm white bread
2 tablespoons butter
1 cup shredded Swiss cheese

Preheat oven to 350 degrees.
1. Mix oil and flour and spread in bottom of greased baking dish.
2. Combine mushrooms, shallots, and tarragon and half the parsley and spread evenly over flour mixture.
3. Drizzle evenly with wine and cream.
4. Arrange fish over top and sprinkle with salt, pepper and paprika.
5. With fork, pull bread apart into crumbs and lightly brown them in butter. Mix with remaining parsley and sprinkle over the fish.
6. Bake uncovered at 350 degrees for 20 minutes. Sprinkle cheese over top and return to oven until melted.

Rolled Sole with Mushrooms

Yield: 4 servings

4 large sole fillets
¹/₄ teaspoon salt
¹/₈ teaspoon pepper
dash paprika
4 teaspoons chopped parsley
5 ounces fresh shrimp, cooked and peeled
1 pound fresh mushrooms, chopped
1 tablespoon butter
1 10³/₄-ounce can cream of mushroom soup
¹/₄ cup water
2 teaspoons sherry

Preheat oven to 400 degrees.
1. Sprinkle sole with salt, pepper, paprika, parsley.
2. Combine shrimp and mushrooms; sauté in melted butter.
3. Spread shrimp mixture over sole; roll up, fasten with toothpicks.
4. Combine soup with water and sherry. Pour over sole.
5. Place in casserole dish and bake at 400 degrees for 20 minutes.

Simple Snapper Fillets with Crab Microwave

Waves of flavor!

Yield: 4 servings

**1 pound snapper fillets
1 pound crabmeat
1 cup crispy croutons
2 tablespoons white wine
¼ cup butter, melted
lemon slices for garnish**

1. Arrange fish fillets in 2-quart Pyrex ring mold, spreading crabmeat on top.
2. Sprinkle with croutons, then wine. Pour on melted butter.
3. Microwave on High 8-9 minutes, covered with wax paper, until snapper appears opaque. Garnish with lemon slices.

Whole Trout or Salmon
Microwave

Sportin' good.

Yield: 1 serving

**whole trout or 8- to 10-ounce salmon
2 tablespoons lemon juice
¼ cup butter, melted**

1. Place fish on fish platter and brush with a mixture of lemon juice and melted butter.
2. Cover cooking dish with plastic wrap. Microwave on High 5-6 minutes for 1 fish, 8-9 minutes for 2 fish.
3. When done, fish flakes easily with a fork. Let stand 5 minutes and serve with rest of lemon butter.

Smashing Swordfish Stroganoff

You'll be amazed!!

Yield: 3 servings

3 swordfish steaks
¼ cup butter
1 large onion, thinly sliced
¼ pound mushrooms, sliced
¼ cup dry white wine
2 teaspoons lemon juice
1 teaspoon salt
1 teaspoon Worcestershire sauce
½ teaspoon Dijon mustard
a dash of pepper
1 ½ cups sour cream
hot cooked spinach noodles, buttered
paprika and chopped parsley

1. Cut fish into strips about ½ × 2-inches.
2. In a wide frying pan, melt butter; add onion and cook until soft.
3. Add mushrooms and cook until limp. Remove onion and mushrooms with slotted spoon and cook fish in juices until firm.
4. Blend wine, lemon juice, salt, Worcestershire sauce, mustard and pepper with sour cream until smooth.
5. Return mushrooms and onions to pan with sour cream mixture. Stir evenly to blend. Lower heat and cook until sour cream is heated; do not boil.

 Serve over spinach noodles, sprinkle with paprika and parsley. Smashing!!

Almond Seafood Casserole

A blend of flavors to tempt you.

Yield: 6 servings

1 7½-ounce can crabmeat
1 5-ounce can shrimp
1 cup finely diced celery
1 tablespoon instant minced onion
1 6-ounce can chow mein noodles
1 cup sliced blanched almonds
½ cup water
2 10¾-ounce cans cream of mushroom soup
croutons

Preheat oven to 375 degrees.
1. Combine crabmeat, shrimp, celery, onion, noodles, and ½ cup of the almonds.
2. Add water to soup. Blend well.
3. Pour soup over crab mixture and toss lightly, but thoroughly.
4. Spoon mixture into 6 greased dishes.
5. Sprinkle remaining ½ cup almonds and croutons over top.
6. Bake at 375 degrees about 25 minutes.

Coquilles Saint Jacques
Lon Hinkle

Lon has learned that one does not simply survive in golf, one must excel! He has won the 1978 New Orleans Open, the 1979 Bing Crosby National Pro-Am, and the World Series of Golf. Lon and his wife, Nancy, enjoy fine food and this recipe will bring glowing reviews.

Yield: 6 servings

6 tablespoons butter or margarine
3 tablespoons flour
¼ teaspoon dry mustard
½ teaspoon lemon peel
½ teaspoon Bon Appetit seasoning
½ teaspoon powdered horseradish
2 teaspoons minced onion
2 cups light cream
1 cup chopped fresh mushrooms
¾ pound fresh scallops
½ pound fresh medium shrimp
about 6 tablespoons seasoned breadcrumbs

Preheat oven to 400 degrees.
1. Melt 4 tablespoons of butter over low heat; add next 6 ingredients; blend well.
2. Add cream; cook, stirring, until thickened. Set aside.
3. Sauté mushrooms in 1 tablespoon butter; remove with slotted spoon and add to cream mixture.
4. Wash scallops and cut in half. Shell, clean, and devein shrimp; cut in half. Sauté both in 1 tablespoon butter; remove with slotted spoon and add to cream mixture.
5. Spoon into 6 ramekin shells or an 8 × 8-inch baking dish. Sprinkle with breadcrumbs.
6. Put in oven at 400 degrees and heat until slightly brown and bubbly, about 5-8 minutes.

Sea Scallop Curry

Yield: 3-4 servings

2 tablespoons butter
2 tablespoons oil
1 pound scallops
2 teaspoons curry powder
¼ cup white vermouth
1 tablespoon lemon juice
1 tablespoon chopped parsley
cooked rice

1. Heat butter and oil in medium skillet.
2. Add scallops and cook for a few minutes, stirring constantly.
3. Sprinkle with curry powder and mix well. Cook a few minutes more.
4. Remove scallops and keep warm. To same skillet, add vermouth, lemon juice and parsley. Stir, scraping brown bits from bottom of pan.
5. Pour sauce over scallops and serve immediately over rice.

Crab Louis in Avocado Halves

Yield: 4 servings

1 egg yolk
2 teaspoons prepared mustard
½ teaspoon Worcestershire sauce
2 teaspoons red wine vinegar
½ cup oil
1 tablespoon chili sauce
¼ cup finely chopped scallions
4 large stuffed green olives, chopped
salt and pepper
1 pound lump crabmeat
4 ripe avocados
lettuce leaves

1. Put yolk in mixing bowl and add mustard, Worcester-shire sauce and vinegar. Beat with wire whisk. Add the oil gradually, beating rapidly.
2. When thickened and smooth, add the chili sauce, scallions and olives. Mix well and season with salt and pepper.
3. Put crab in a mixing bowl and add half the sauce. Mix gently.
4. Split the avocados in half and discard the pits. Pile equal portions of the crab into the avocado halves. Spoon remaining sauce over.
5. Serve on lettuce leaves.

Shrimp Casserole   Marty Fleckman

Marty no longer travels on tour; he enjoys living in Houston, Texas. This recipe is messy and delicious! Serve with French bread to dip in the butter mixture, salad and your favorite wine.

Yield: 4 servings

2 pounds large shrimp, headed, with shells
3 tablespoons cracked pepper
2 teaspoons salt
3 large cloves garlic, pressed or finely chopped
¼-½ cup butter

Preheat oven to 350 degrees.
1. In casserole dish, put layer of shrimp, pepper, salt, garlic. Continue until all is used.
2. Put in refrigerator, covered, for several hours.
3. Remove, uncover, and put butter on top in pats and bake at 350 degrees about 15 minutes or until shrimp turn pink; stir or baste twice.

Shrimp Creole   Johnny Pott

Johnny and his wife, Mary Rose, traveled widely when he was on tour. They now live at the Carmel Valley Ranch, Carmel, California. When their friends come to visit, they often prepare this wonderful Creole dish. Make it ahead and enjoy your company.

Yield: 10 servings

½ cup flour
½ cup vegetable oil
2 cups chopped onion
1 cup chopped green pepper
1 cup chopped celery with leaves
2 cloves garlic, chopped
2 6-ounce cans tomato paste
1 16-ounce can tomatoes
3 cups water
3 teaspoons salt
½ teaspoon red pepper
5 pounds raw, deveined, peeled shrimp
2 tablespoons chopped green onion
2 tablespoons chopped parsley

1. In a large heavy pot, make a roux (brown over slow heat, stirring constantly) of flour and oil.
2. Add onions, green pepper, celery and garlic and cook until soft.
3. Add tomato paste and tomatoes; mix and cook about 5 minutes.
4. Add water and salt and pepper.
5. Add shrimp and cook about 10 minutes longer.

This recipe is best when prepared several hours before serving. Let stand so that flavors can blend.

 Reheat and serve over rice with French bread.

Add onion tops and parsley 5 minutes before serving.

Herbed Shrimp   Microwave

Lovely for a light lunch.

Yield: 2 cups

½ cup butter or margarine
½ teaspoon tarragon
⅛ teaspoon celery salt
dash pepper
½ cup chopped parsley
2 cups cooked shrimp

1. In a 1½-quart glass casserole, place butter, tarragon, celery salt, pepper and parsley.
2. Microwave on High for 1 to 2 minutes or until melted.
3. Stir in shrimp. Microwave on Medium, covered, for 1 to 2 minutes or until shrimp is heated, stirring once. Do not boil shrimp.

Creamed Jalapeño Shrimp in Patty Shells   Mark Coward

A real firecracker!! The Mark Cowards created this recipe…a colorful combination of shrimp, peas and onions.

Yield: 6 servings

1 package frozen Pepperidge Farm patty shells
1 10-ounce can cream of shrimp soup
⅓ cup milk
¼ teaspoon dill weed (optional)
1 10-ounce package frozen shrimp (pre-cooked)
1 10-ounce package frozen green peas and pearl onions
jalapeño juice to taste

1. Bake patty shells as directed on package.
2. Combine soup, milk, and dill weed; heat over low heat until sauce simmers.
3. Add shrimp, peas, onions, and juice and heat.
4. Fill patty shells and serve.

Cold Shrimp-Stuffed Avocado   Hale Irwin

First rate all the way!! Hale is one of the finest guys on tour and always seems to keep a good round going. He has the skill to make impossible shots for sparkling victories. Hale, who graduated from the University of Colorado and turned professional in 1968, won the 1984 Crosby Pro-Am.

Yield: 4 servings

1 pound fresh shrimp, cooked, cleaned and chopped
1 cup finely chopped onion
2 teaspoons lemon juice
3 tablespoons vinegar-and-oil salad dressing
^{2}/$_3$ cup Hellmann's mayonnaise
1 ^{1}/$_2$ teaspoons Shedd's Old Style Sauce
^{1}/$_2$ teaspoon freshly ground black pepper
^{1}/$_4$ teaspoon Beau Monde seasoning
^{1}/$_4$ teaspoon seasoning salt
^{1}/$_2$ teaspoon dill weed (optional)
2 ripe avocados, halved

Mix all ingredients together and stuff into avocado halves.

Enjoy!

Hot Shrimp-Stuffed Avocado

John R. Geertsen, Jr.

This unusual dish always achieved acclaim whenever John and his wife served it during the many years they were affiliated with the Monterey Peninsula Country Club in Pebble Beach. The avocados show off the shrimp to its best advantage.

Yield: 4 servings

¹/₂ cup chopped celery
¹/₂ cup chopped green pepper
2 tablespoons butter
2 8-ounce cans tomato sauce
1 tablespoon instant minced onion
¹/₂ teaspoon salt
¹/₂ teaspoon sugar
¹/₈ teaspoon pepper
1 tablespoon lime juice
1 ¹/₂ cups cooked and cleaned shrimp
3 avocados

1. Sauté celery and green pepper in butter over low heat, stirring occasionally, for 5 minutes.
2. Add tomato sauce and onion; simmer 20 minutes.
3. Stir in salt, sugar, pepper, lime juice and shrimp. Heat until steaming hot.
4. Cut 3 avocados (at room temperature) in halves, lengthwise, removing pits, and sprinkle with lime juice and salt.
5. Spoon hot shrimp mixture into cavities of avocados and serve at once.

Oysters Alexandria   Low Fat

Touching on the sea.

Yield: 4 servings (137 calories each)

2 dozen oysters, drained, liquid reserved
1 tablespoon oil
1 onion, finely chopped
½ green pepper, chopped
2 cups stewed tomatoes
1 tablespoon vinegar
1 teaspoon sugar
¼ teaspoon Accent
pinch oregano
salt and pepper to taste

1. Cook oysters for not more than 1 minute in ¼-cup of the oyster liquid. Remove oysters.
2. Heat oil with 1 tablespoon oyster liquid in skillet. Place onion and pepper in skillet and simmer for 3 to 5 minutes, then add tomatoes, vinegar, sugar and seasonings and continue cooking for 15 to 20 minutes.
3. Stir several times during cooking.
4. Add oysters to sauce and cook for not more than 1 minute. Above recipe may be served on toast points, if desired. Add 75 calories for each slice.

OOOOOOOOOOOOOOOOOOOOOO

Poultry

OOOOOOOOOOOOOOOOOOOOO

Breast of Chicken on Rice

Ralph Landrum

A simple and delicious favorite recipe of Mary Pat and
Ralph's, it will probably become yours, too. All that is
needed is a green salad and a glass of wine for a quick and
easy supper.

Yield: 2-3 servings

1 10³/₄-ounce can cream of mushroom soup
1 soup can of milk
³/₄ cup uncooked rice
1 4-ounce can mushroom stems and pieces
1 envelope (about 1 ¹/₂ ounces) dry onion soup mix
2 chicken breasts, split in half

Preheat oven to 350 degrees.
1. Blend soup and milk.
2. Stir together half of the soup mixture, rice, mushrooms
   with liquid, and half of the onion soup mix.
3. Pour into an ungreased 11 × 7 × 2-inch baking dish.
4. Arrange chicken breasts on rice mixture. Pour remaining
   soup mixture over chicken and sprinkle with remaining
   onion soup mix.
5. Cover and bake 1 hour at 350 degrees. Uncover and
   bake 15 minutes longer.

Chicken Divan   Mike Sullivan

Serve this to your favorite foursome. Mike has considerable potential and now that back problems have passed, he can get on with his game. Sandy and Mike live in Florida and love flying and fishing. Mike won the 1980 Southern Open.

Yield: 4 servings

1/4 **cup mayonnaise**
1/4 **cup sour cream**
1 10³/4-ounce can cream of chicken soup
2 tablespoons lemon juice
1 bunch fresh broccoli, cut up and steamed 8-10
    minutes
4 chicken breasts, cooked and boned
3/4 **cup grated medium Cheddar cheese**
1 cup stuffing mix
1/4 **cup melted butter**

Preheat oven to 350 degrees.
1. Mix mayonnaise, sour cream, soup and lemon juice.
2. Line a greased casserole with broccoli and add chicken.
3. Pour sauce over all and sprinkle with cheese.
4. Mix stuffing and butter and spread on top.
5. Bake 30 minutes at 350 degrees. Cover first 15 minutes, then uncover for the last 15 minutes.

Chicken with Eggplant

An interesting combination of flavors.

Yield: 4 servings

1 3-pound chicken, cut into quarters
salt to taste
freshly ground pepper to taste
2 small eggplants
1 large onion
2 small tomatoes
2 tablespoons olive oil
1 tablespoon finely minced garlic
½ cup red wine vinegar
½ cup white wine
½ cup chicken broth
1 bay leaf
¼ teaspoon dried thyme
salt and pepper to taste
¼ teaspoon dried hot red pepper flakes
chopped parsley for garnish

1. Sprinkle chicken pieces with salt and pepper. Set aside.
2. Trim ends off eggplants. Cut lengthwise in half and cut each half lengthwise into three long slices. Cut slices crosswise into inch pieces. There should be about 5 cups.
3. Cut onion into very thin slices. There should be about a cup.
4. Cut cores from tomatoes. Cut tomatoes into inch cubes or slightly smaller. There should be about 1½ cups.
5. Heat oil in large skillet and add chicken pieces, skin side down. Cook about 5 minutes on one side and turn, cooking 5 minutes more. Transfer chicken to platter.
6. Add eggplant, onions, and garlic to skillet. Cook, stirring, about 1 minute and add tomatoes. Stir.
7. Add vinegar, wine and broth and bring to boil. Stir. Add bay leaf, thyme, salt, pepper and pepper flakes. Stir and return chicken to the skillet. Turn pieces in sauce.
8. Cover loosely and let cook, basting occasionally, about 20 minutes or until chicken is done. Remove bay leaf.

 Serve with sauce poured over and sprinkle with parsley.

Rub the insides of chicken with a little lemon juice. This tenderizes as well as sweetens.

Two Cans and One Box!

Cindy Hill

A Phi Beta Kappa from the University of Miami, Cindy has blended together two cans and one box for a quick and easy entrée. Now you can spend the extra time practicing your putting!

Yield: 4 servings

1 10¾-ounce can cream of mushroom soup
1 10¾-ounce can cream of chicken soup
1 can of water
1 box Uncle Ben's long-grain rice
2 chicken breasts, halved

Preheat oven to 300 degrees.
1. Combine soup, water, rice (including seasoning) in cooking dish.
2. Place chicken in dish; cook, uncovered, for 2 hours at 300 degrees.

Elegant Easy Chicken

Clarence Rose

"Par-tee" chicken. Clarence was born in Goldsboro, North Carolina, and attended Clemson University. Chicken is often on the menu at Jan and Clarence's home.

Yield: 6 servings

¼ cup white wine
1 10¾-ounce can cream of chicken soup
6 chicken breast halves, skinned
6 slices Swiss cheese
¼ to ½ cup seasoned breadcrumbs
¼ cup butter, melted

Preheat oven to 350 degrees.
1. Mix wine and soup together.
2. Place chicken in shallow baking dish. Pour sauce over chicken.
3. Top each with one slice of Swiss cheese.
4. Sprinkle with breadcrumbs.
5. Pour butter over chicken. Bake at 350 degrees for 1 hour, uncovered.

Bill's Chicken Enchiladas
Bill Rogers

A great "birdie" dish. Now that Bill's family has increased with the birth of his daughter, he has a very positive attitude towards everything. His winnings include the 1981 World Series of Golf.

Yield: 14 servings

1 10¾-ounce can cream of mushroom soup
1 10¾-ounce can cream of chicken soup
1 4-ounce can chopped green chilies
1 16-ounce carton sour cream
1 20-ounce package flour tortillas
1 chicken, cooked, boned, and broken into pieces, white meat preferred
1 pound Cheddar cheese, grated
1 pound Monterey Jack cheese, grated
1 bunch green onions, chopped

Preheat oven to 300 degrees.
1. In large bowl, mix the soups, chilies, and sour cream.
2. Spread mixture on flour tortillas.
3. In equal proportions, sprinkle on chicken, cheeses, and green onions.
4. Roll tortillas and put in greased baking pan.
5. Sprinkle remainder of cheeses on top; if there is any remaining sauce, that, too, can go on top of the tortillas before baking. Bake at 300 degrees until bubbly, about 30 minutes.

Doug's Favorite Chicken Enchiladas   Doug Tewell

A real crowd pleaser. Everybody loves enchiladas and leftover chicken can be used for this recipe. Doug is one of the more inspiring pros. Due to hard work and discipline, he is one of the game's better players.

Yield: 8-10 servings

1 medium onion, chopped
2 tablespoons butter
1 cup chicken broth
1 10¾-ounce can cream of mushroom soup
1 10¾-ounce can cream of chicken soup
1 4-ounce can green chilies, chopped
1 3-pound frying chicken, cooked and boned
1 package (12) tortillas
1 pound Longhorn cheese, grated

Preheat oven to 350 degrees.
1. Brown onion in butter and add broth, soups, chilies and chicken pieces.
2. In a 9 × 13-inch baking dish, layer tortillas, chicken sauce and cheese. Bake in a 350-degree oven for 40 minutes or until bubbly.

Q Can be made early and refrigerated until needed.

Chicken and Spinach Enchiladas   Lanny Wadkins

Powerfully good! Another version of enchiladas. Lanny and Penelope live in Dallas, Texas, and enjoy casual entertaining. His approach to a game of golf is quite simple—he attacks the course with each calculated shot!

Yield: 10 or more servings

4 1/2-5 pound chicken
3 pints sour cream
2 large onions, chopped
2 tablespoons butter
salt
2 10-ounce packages frozen chopped spinach
   (cooked, drained)
4 4-ounce cans green chilies
1/2 cup milk
20 soft flour tortillas
10 ounces Monterey Jack cheese, grated

Preheat oven to 350 degrees.
1. Cook chicken until tender. Debone and chop into small pieces.
2. Make sauce of sour cream, onions sautéed in butter, salt, spinach, chilies and milk. Mix with the chicken.
3. Fill tortillas and fold into thirds.
4. Place in baking dishes, fold side down, and cover with grated cheese. Top with remaining sauce.
5. Bake at 350 degrees for 30 minutes or until done.

Q   May be refrigerated or frozen after baking.

Chicken Fantastic   Microwave
Bobby Clampett

Such an easy way to serve chicken. Bobby lives in Florida, but grew up in the Monterey Peninsula. A favorite son and budding young star, he will shine for many years. Bobby and his wife, Ann, enjoy this interesting chicken dish.

Yield: 4-6 servings

3-4 chicken breasts, split
1 8-ounce jar Russian salad dressing
1 12-ounce jar apricot preserves
1 package dry onion soup mix

1. Arrange chicken in a 12 × 7½-inch glass dish.
2. Combine dressing, preserves and soup mix in medium bowl; spoon sauce over chicken.
3. Set microwave oven on Medium, cover dish with waxed paper; cook for 17-20 minutes. Rotate dish one-half through cooking time.

Bob Hope's Favorite
Chicken Hash   Bob Hope

Bob is never very far from golf. Although he travels extensively, he does manage to play a few rounds each week. The Bob Hope Classic is held in Palm Springs each year.

Yield: 2 servings

2 chicken breasts, cooked
2 strips of bacon, cooked till crisp
½ small onion
salt and pepper
½ teaspoon lemon juice
2 tablespoons butter
2 tablespoons sour cream
1 teaspoon dry sherry wine

1. Cut chicken in fine strips, crumble bacon and combine with the onion, seasonings and lemon juice.
2. Sauté until thoroughly heated in the butter, and shortly before serving add the sour cream and sherry. Do not allow to cook after adding the two last ingredients. Just heat through.

Chicken Florentine Jack Nicklaus

When Barbara and Jack graciously entertain in their lovely home in North Palm Beach, Florida, they often serve chicken and this is one of their favorites.

Yield: 6 servings

6 chicken breast halves, boned and cut in pieces
salt and pepper to taste
1/4 cup butter
2 tablespoons oil
2 10-ounce packages frozen chopped spinach*
1/2 cup mayonnaise
1/4 cup sour cream
1 10¾-ounce can cream of chicken soup
1 tablespoon lemon juice
1 teaspoon curry powder
1/2 cup grated sharp cheese
1/2 cup cornflake crumbs

Preheat oven to 350 degrees.
1. Sauté slightly salted and peppered chicken pieces in butter and oil for 10 minutes.
2. Cook spinach. Drain and squeeze dry.
3. Spread spinach in bottom of a 2-quart casserole. Top with chicken.
4. Mix mayonnaise, sour cream, soup, lemon juice and curry powder. Pour over chicken. Sprinkle with cheese.
5. Top with crumbs. Bake at 350 degrees for 25 minutes.

*For variety, substitute broccoli for spinach.

Hole-in-One Chicken
Clint Eastwood

One of Pebble Beach's most famous residents, Clint owns the Hog's Breath Restaurant and is an avid golfer. This Hole-in-One is a cinch to make!

Yield: 1 serving

½ whole chicken
2-3 tablespoons butter
1 tablespoon oil
½ cup sliced mushrooms
3 green onions, finely sliced
⅓ cup Madeira wine
1 medium tomato, diced

Preheat oven to 350 degrees.
1. Roast chicken, covered, for 1 hour at 350 degrees. Let cool.
2. Remove skin, debone and cut into bite-sized pieces. Lightly sauté in the butter and oil in skillet.
3. Pour in Madeira and flame it. Add mushrooms and onions.
4. Cook 3 minutes over medium heat; let simmer 3-4 minutes.
5. Garnish with diced tomatoes.

Lime-Cucumber-Dill Chicken

Barry Jaeckel

Barry and Evelyn Jaeckel live in Palm Desert, California, and enjoy this light way to cook chicken. Barry is a consistent player, always working on his swing. A graduate of Santa Monica College, his special interests are sports, especially UCLA basketball.

Yield: 6 servings

6 chicken breasts, skinned and boned
salt
pepper
juice of 1 lime
1 teaspoon dill weed
1 green pepper, diced
1 8-ounce bottle creamy cucumber salad dressing
lemon or lime slices for garnish

Preheat oven to 350 degrees.
1. Season chicken breasts with salt and pepper to taste.
2. Place in a 13 × 9-inch baking dish.
3. Sprinkle lime juice and dill weed over chicken. Bake 30 minutes at 350 degrees.
4. Remove chicken from oven. Sprinkle green pepper over chicken and spread dressing generously over all.
5. Return chicken to oven and continue baking another 15 minutes.
6. Remove and serve hot. Sauce from the pan may be served on the side. Serve with white rice. Add lemon or lime atop each serving for garnish.

Italian Chicken   Patti Rizzo

Try Patti's easy Italian chicken when you have unexpected guests. It's quick and always popular. Patti likes to serve it with spaghetti, tossed salad and red wine. Patti joined the LPGA tour in 1982, after a spectacular amateur career. She easily claimed Rookie of the Year in 1982.

Yield: 4 servings

4 chicken breasts with wings attached
salt and pepper
butter
8-ounce bottle Wishbone Italian salad dressing

Preheat oven to 375 degrees.
1. Wash chicken breasts and place them bone side up in pan.
2. Sprinkle salt and pepper and spread butter on top of all breasts.
3. Pour Italian dressing (approximately ⅓ bottle) over the chicken.
4. Broil for 10 minutes. Turn chicken over and repeat the seasonings.
5. Return to oven and bake at 375 degrees for 15 to 20 minutes.

Marinated Chicken Véronique
Amy Alcott

Never misses!! Always a winner, Amy is already an LPGA millionaire. She joined the tour in 1975, moving up through the amateur ranks. She enjoys working with youngsters, donating her free time to many charity classics. She is the 1983 winner of the Nabisco Dinah Shore Invitational.

Marinade

2 tablespoons cornstarch
3 tablespoons dry sherry
1 tablespoon soy sauce
½ teaspoon powdered ginger

4 chicken breast halves, skinned and boned
¾ pound red or green grapes
2 tablespoons butter or margarine
2 tablespoons oil
¼ cup water
1¼ cups whipping cream or half & half
parsley

1. Combine cornstarch, sherry, soy sauce and ginger to make marinade.
2. Cut chicken breast halves diagonally into 4 or 5 strips. Put in bowl with prepared marinade. Let stand 5 minutes.
3. Halve the grapes and seed, if necessary; set aside.
4. Heat butter and oil in skillet. Remove chicken from marinade, reserving marinade and sauté quickly, 2 minutes per side.
5. Remove chicken and keep warm.
6. Deglaze pan with ¼ cup water on high heat. Stir cream into remaining marinade in bowl; then pour mixture into pan.
7. Cook and stir over medium heat to thicken slightly. Put chicken and grapes into sauce. Heat through. Pour into heated bowl.

 Garnish with parsley and serve with rice.

Oriental Chicken   Mike Gove

After golf, Wok-a-round of veggies!! Mike and Carrie believe
in good, natural food and both enjoy puttering in the
kitchen. Serve this with rice and sourdough rolls for a
good, nutritious meal. Mike turned professional in 1980.
He was a 1979 Walker Cup team member. (See photograph)

Yield: 4 servings

4 skinned, boned and cubed chicken breasts
1/2 cup soy sauce
4-6 tablespoons peanut oil
2 cups slant-cut celery pieces
2 cups chopped broccoli
2 cups snow peas
1 cup fresh mushrooms, chopped
2 cups bean sprouts
1/2 teaspoon rosemary
1/3 cup water
2-3 tablespoons soy sauce, to taste
1-2 tablespoons Worcestershire sauce, to taste
1-2 tablespoons cornstarch, as needed

1. Soak chicken cubes in soy sauce overnight.
2. In heated wok*, at 350 degrees, stir-fry chicken in
   peanut oil. When chicken is tender and white, remove
   or push to sides of wok.
3. Stir-fry celery, broccoli and snow peas 2-3 minutes. Add
   mushrooms and sprouts and stir-fry 2-3 minutes longer.
   Sprinkle with rosemary.
4. Reduce heat to 250 degrees. Push vegetables to side of
   wok or remove. In center of wok, combine water, soy
   sauce, Worcestershire sauce and cornstarch, stirring
   until thickened.
5. Toss chicken and vegetables back in sauce and serve
   over rice.

   Easy recipe to increase or decrease.

 For crunchy vegetables, stir-fry. For softer vegetables,
cover and steam.

   *For best results, use an electric wok.

Pepperidge Farm Chicken Breasts   Jack Doss

A "cinch" to make. Jack is the professional at Pasatiempo Golf Club, Santa Cruz, California.

Yield: 4 servings

4 chicken breasts
melted butter
Pepperidge Farm crumb stuffing
an oven

Preheat oven to 325 degrees.
1. Dip chicken breasts in melted butter.
2. Roll in finely crushed Pepperidge Farm crumb stuffing.
3. Bake at 325 degrees for one hour.

Phony Abalone

You can't tell the difference!!

Yield: 2 servings

2 chicken breasts, skinned, boned, butterflied
1 8-ounce bottle clam juice
2 eggs, beaten
about ½ cup Italian-seasoned breadcrumbs

1. Pound chicken breasts lightly. Marinate in the clam juice overnight, in refrigerator.
2. Drain the chicken breasts. Dip in egg, then in the bread-crumbs.
3. Preheat pan over medium-high heat with enough oil to cover bottom.
4. Sauté chicken no more than two minutes per side.

 Serve with lemon wedge and tartar sauce.

Rolled Chicken Breasts

John Fought, Jr.

This could be a trophy winner! John turned professional in 1977 after graduation from Brigham Young University. He and his wife, Donna, enjoy small groups of friends for dinner and this is a delightful entrée. They now live in Portland, Oregon.

Yield: 8-10 servings

12 chicken breasts, boned and halved
12 thin slices ham
12 slices Swiss cheese
2-3 eggs, beaten
butter or oil for browning
seasoned flour (season according to personal taste)
¼-½ cup white wine
1 or 2 10¾-ounce cans cream of chicken soup

1. Remove skin and small white tendon on underside of each half breast. Place breasts between 2 pieces of waxed paper and pound flat.
2. Place slice of ham and slice of cheese on chicken breast, roll and secure together with a toothpick.
3. Dip the 12 rolled breasts, one at a time, in beaten egg, then in seasoned flour, coating each one completely.
4. Place breasts in greased fry pan and brown. Add ¼ to ½ cup white wine and brown at high temperature for a couple of minutes.
5. Add chicken soup with a *small* amount of water (approximately ½ cup to each can of soup used). Put lid on and simmer for about an hour.

Deviled Chicken Wings   Mick Soli

A first-flight recipe to serve when you are with friends around the barbecue. A wonderful finger food for a casual meal. Mike was born in Missouri and now lives in Spring, Texas. He joined the tour in 1979.

Yield: 6 servings

1 medium onion, chopped (about ³/₄-cup)
¹/₃ cup red wine vinegar
¹/₄ cup prepared Dijon-style mustard
3 tablespoons olive oil
3 cloves garlic, minced
1 tablespoon dried rosemary, crushed
¹/₂ teaspoon salt
¹/₃ teaspoon pepper
5¹/₂ pounds chicken wings (6 wings per serving)

1. In large bowl, combine onion, vinegar, mustard, oil, garlic, rosemary, salt and pepper; mix well.
2. Pierce chicken wings with fork. Add wings to marinade. Cover; refrigerate 5 hours or overnight. Stir wings often to distribute marinade.
3. Place wings on barbecue over medium high heat.
4. Cook 10 minutes on one side; turn and brush with marinade and continue cooking 10 minutes longer or until wings are cooked through.

Roast Almond Duck

An Oriental delicacy.

Yield: 2-4 servings

1 cup (or less) soy sauce
2 tablespoons honey
1 teaspoon Spice Islands Orange Peel
1-2 cloves garlic, crushed or pressed
1 4- to 5-pound duck
1 cup sweet rice (Mochi Gome)
1 cup almonds, split in halves, or 1 teaspoon almond
extract
2 tablespoons peanut oil

Preheat oven to 300 degrees.
1. Heat soy sauce and honey slowly in saucepan; add orange peel and garlic. Heat until sauce becomes slightly thickened.
2. Cool sauce, spread on duck evenly, inside and outside. Refrigerate overnight.
3. Cook rice with almonds until rice is fluffy. Stuff duck with rice. Truss.
4. Heat peanut oil in frying pan. Fry duck in pan until light brown, turning to brown all sides.
5. Roast in preheated 300-degree oven for 2 to 2½ hours.
6. Chop duck lengthwise, then crosswise into 1-inch pieces.

♀ Serve on bed of lettuce; garnish with Chinese parsley.

Roast Pheasant Vermouth

A very pleasant pheasant!

Yield: 4 servings

3 tablespoons butter
3 green onions, chopped
1 3-ounce can mushrooms, drained
¼ cup pecans, chopped
1 apple, chopped
¾ cup breadcrumbs
salt and pepper
dry vermouth
1 pheasant, cleaned
½ cup butter
1 cup dry vermouth

Preheat oven to 300 degrees.
1. Melt butter, add onions and mushrooms. Sauté until onions are tender.
2. Add pecans, apple, breadcrumbs, seasonings and enough vermouth to bind together.
3. Stuff pheasant with breadcrumb mixture and place in roasting pan.
4. Melt butter, mix with 1 cup of vermouth and pour over bird.
5. Roast at 300 degrees, for 1 hour, basting frequently. Pour sauce over pheasant before serving.

♀ Slow cooking is important to keep the bird moist.

Pheasant Stew   Craig Stadler

A Million Dollar Winner, Craig won the 1982 Masters. He and his family live in Tahoe, California. Craig has learned to be patient, control his emotions and work hard. These qualities contribute to successes in other interests as well. When Craig goes hunting and shoots a pheasant, he uses this recipe for a delicious stew.

Yield: 4-6 servings

1 pheasant, cleaned
1 small onion, chopped
1/2 cup chopped celery
3-4 carrots, scraped and cut into slices
1 medium zucchini, sliced
1/2 cabbage, cut into pieces
1/2 cup chopped celery (in addition to above amount)
1 cup peeled and cubed potatoes
1/2 cup chopped onion
salt and garlic powder to taste
2-3 chicken bouillon cubes
dumplings

1. Cover pheasant in large stew pot with water.
2. Cook with small onion and 1/2 cup celery for 1 1/2 hours.
3. Remove bones from pheasant and cut meat into pieces.
4. Return meat to soup and add carrots, zucchini, cabbage, celery, potatoes, and onion.
5. Boil gently for another 1 to 1 1/2 hours.
6. Cook dumplings and add to stew at the end.
7. Season with salt, garlic and 2-3 chicken bouillon cubes.

Country Club Turkey   Microwave

Simply elegant.

Yield: 4 servings

**2 10-ounce packages frozen asparagus spears,
thawed
1 10¾-ounce can cream of chicken soup
2 cups cooked, cubed turkey
½ cup sliced, pitted, ripe olives
½ cup diced pimento
½ teaspoon grated onion
⅛ teaspoon nutmeg
¼ cup shredded smokey cheese**

1. Place asparagus in a 12 × 7-inch glass dish. Cover with
   plastic wrap; pierce a hole to allow steam to escape.
   Microwave on High for 5 to 7 minutes or until partially
   cooked.
2. Drain, and arrange spears evenly in dish. Set aside.
3. Combine soup, turkey, olives, pimento, onion, and
   nutmeg. Spoon over asparagus.
4. Top with cheese. Microwave on Medium, uncovered,
   for 11 to 13 minutes, or until heated through.

Chinese Chicken with Vegetables Low Fat

An incentive to count calories.

Yield: 6 servings (154 calories each)

1 pound skinless, boneless chicken breasts
8 tablespoons vegetable oil
2 cups 2-inch cubes of green or red peppers
1 cup thinly sliced mushrooms
4 thin slices ginger
1 ½ cups pineapple pieces, preferably fresh
1 ½ tablespoons cornstarch
⅔ cup unsalted chicken broth or pineapple juice

1. Cut the chicken into 1-inch cubes.
2. Heat 6 tablespoons of oil in a wok and add the chicken. Cook, stirring, until it loses its raw look, about 1 minute.
3. Remove the chicken, leaving the oil in the wok. Add the remaining oil. When hot again, add the peppers, mushrooms and ginger. Cook, stirring, for about 2 minutes.
4. Add the pineapple and chicken and cook, stirring, for about 2 minutes.
5. Blend the cornstarch with the broth and stir it into the mixture.
6. Cook for 2 minutes or until thickened. Serve hot with unsalted rice.

Chicken Marsala   Microwave/Low Fat

It's great...try it!!

Yield: 6 servings (270 calories each)

3 pounds chicken pieces
1 cup Italian-seasoned breadcrumbs
1 teaspoon oregano
¼ teaspoon dill weed
2 tablespoons fresh parsley
2 tablespoons paprika
½ teaspoon garlic powder
½ cup Marsala wine
1 15-ounce can peeled, whole tomatoes
1 cup sliced fresh mushrooms

1. Wash chicken thoroughly. Combine breadcrumbs, oregano, dill weed, parsley, paprika, and garlic powder and place in plastic bag.
2. Shake 1 or 2 pieces of chicken at a time in the breadcrumb mixture. Place pieces of chicken in casserole dish. Put smaller pieces with less meat toward the middle. Drizzle part of the Marsala on the chicken to moisten.
3. Bake on High in microwave for 15 minutes, uncovered.
4. Add the Marsala, tomatoes and then the mushrooms. Cook for an additional 15 minutes. Rotate dish midway through the cooking.
5. Allow to stand for 10 minutes before serving.

Turkey Stroganoff   Low Fat

Yield: 8 servings (178 calories each)

2 tablespoons corn oil margarine
2 cups sliced mushrooms
1 medium onion, thinly sliced
3 tablespoons flour
2 1/2 cups chicken or turkey stock
1 tablespoon tomato paste
1/2 teaspoon paprika
1/2 teaspoon dried basil
1/4 teaspoon nutmeg
3 tablespoons sherry
4 cups julienne-cut cooked turkey
3/4 cup sour cream

1. Melt 1 tablespoon of the margarine in a large skillet. Add the mushrooms and onion and cook until tender, about 5 minutes.
2. Remove the mushrooms and onions. Melt the remaining tablespoon of margarine in the same skillet. Add the flour and cook, stirring, until the flour is lightly browned, about 3 minutes.
3. In a saucepan, bring the stock to a boil and add it to the flour mixture, stirring constantly to form a smooth sauce.
4. Add the tomato paste, paprika, basil, nutmeg, and sherry and simmer for 10 minutes. Add the turkey, mushrooms and onions to the pan and simmer 10 more minutes.
5. Add the sour cream and mix thoroughly. Serve immediately, over noodles.

Vegetables

Artichokes with Peppered Butter Sauce   Microwave

Yield: 4 servings

4 artichokes
1 tablespoon lemon juice
$1/2$ teaspoon salt
1 $1/4$ cups water
$1/2$ teaspoon butter

Sauce

$1/2$ cup butter
$1/2$ teaspoon salt
$1/2$ teaspoon black pepper

1. Trim the tips of the outer artichoke leaves, using kitchen scissors. Wash the artichokes under cold running water.
2. Combine the lemon juice, salt and water in a large dish and add the butter. Microwave on High for 3 to 4 minutes.
3. Place the artichokes upright in the dish, cover and microwave on High for 12 to 15 minutes until the lower leaves can be pulled away from the stem easily. Let stand, covered, while preparing the sauce.
4. Place the butter, salt, and pepper in a small serving jug and microwave on High for 1 $1/2$ minutes, or until melted.
5. Transfer the artichokes to serving plates with a slotted spoon. Serve the sauce separately.

Asparagus Casserole Larry Nelson

With each passing year, more sports enthusiasts are coming to know of Larry, who won the 1983 United States Open. Larry and his wife, Gayle, are Georgia residents and offer warm Southern hospitality, especially with this casserole.

Yield: 6 servings

1 10¾-ounce can cream of mushroom soup
½ cup milk, whole or evaporated
1 10-ounce can asparagus, extra tender spears
½ cup pecans, chopped
1 hard-cooked egg, finely chopped
1 cup Saltine cracker crumbs
1 cup grated Cheddar cheese

Preheat oven to 350 degrees.
1. Heat soup and milk in saucepan. Drain asparagus and add to soup. Break up spears and mix well. Set aside.
2. Butter a 1½-quart casserole.
3. Pour ½ of soup mixture into casserole, sprinkle with pecans and chopped egg. Scatter a small amount of cracker crumbs and cheese.
4. Layer with remainder of soup mixture and top with cracker crumbs and finally, cheese.
5. Bake in a 350-degree oven for 20-25 minutes.

Sweet and Sour Asparagus

Mark Coward

An interesting way to serve asparagus. No muss, no fuss! A zesty combination to prepare in advance and serve cold. Mark joined the PGA tour in 1983.

Yield: 4 servings

²/₃ cup white vinegar
¹/₂ cup sugar
¹/₂ teaspoon salt
1 teaspoon whole cloves
3 sticks cinnamon
1 tablespoon celery seed
¹/₂ cup water
2 16-ounce cans all green asparagus or 3 pounds cooked fresh
1 hard-cooked egg, grated

1. Mix vinegar, sugar, salt, and spices in a saucepan with water. Bring to a boil.
2. Place asparagus in a flat baking dish and pour boiling liquid over it. Cover and store in the refrigerator for 24 hours.
3. To serve, pour off liquid and sprinkle with hard-cooked egg.

Baked Beans   Mark Coward

Complete in itself. When friends are going to have a picnic supper and you offer to bring the beans—try this recipe. Mark, born and raised in Austin, Texas, enjoys cooking and this recipe is one of his favorites. Great for a Texas barbecue.

Yield: 20 servings

1 pound hamburger meat
2 onions, finely chopped
¼ cup margarine
2 31-ounce cans pork and beans
3 16-ounce cans Ranch Style beans
¼ cup prepared mustard
1 cup brown sugar
¼ cup maple syrup
1 cup catsup

Preheat oven to 300 degrees.
1. Brown the meat and onions in the margarine.
2. Mix all other ingredients together and bake in a 300-degree oven for one hour or simmer slowly on top of stove until bubbly.

Bean Spice Casserole
John R. Geertsen, Jr.

John is the golf professional at Riverside Country Club, Provo, Utah, where he helps many of the budding young golfers at Brigham Young University. This bean recipe is wonderful for picnics or beach parties!

2 1-pound cans pork and beans
1 12-ounce bottle catsup
1 12-ounce can chunk pineapple, drained
1 medium onion, chopped
1 medium green pepper, chopped
1 cup brown sugar
6 teaspoons Worcestershire sauce
6 weiners, cut in chunks
½ pound bacon, cut in 1-inch pieces and fried to remove grease

Preheat oven to 250 degrees or 325 degrees (see below).
1. Mix all ingredients together in greased Pyrex dish or casserole.
2. Bake 3 hours at 250 degrees or 2 hours at 325 degrees.

Green Bean Casserole

Payne Stewart

In his plus fours, argyle socks and cap, Payne has become the most colorful dresser on the tour. After a two-year stint on the Asian tour, he is now proving himself a real professional.

Yield: 4 servings

1 10¾-ounce can cream of mushroom soup
6 ounces hot pepper cheese, grated (more or less, to suit one's taste)
1 15-ounce can French-style green beans
1 16-ounce can fried onion rings

Preheat oven to 350 degrees.
1. Blend soup with cheese.
2. Mix soup and cheese mixture with green beans in greased casserole dish.
3. Sprinkle onions on top of mixture and bake at 350 degrees for 30 minutes.

Broccoli Casserole   Tom Watson

Tom, a graduate of Stanford University, has achieved many goals. He has been Player of the Year for five years. We all remember how he pitched in at the 17th green at Pebble Beach to win the United States Open in 1982. Tom and his wife, Linda, love to entertain in their home in Mission Hills, Kansas.

Yield: 6 servings

**2 10-ounce packages frozen chopped broccoli,
   cooked and drained
1 10¾-ounce can cream of mushroom soup
2 eggs
4 ounces sharp Cheddar cheese, grated
¾ cup mayonnaise
1 medium onion, chopped
½ cup Ritz cracker crumbs
2 tablespoons butter**

Preheat oven to 350 degrees.
1. Mix together all ingredients except the cracker crumbs.
2. Pour into a well-buttered 8 × 8-inch baking dish.
3. Sprinkle cracker crumbs on top and dot with butter.
4. Bake at 350 degrees for approximately 30 minutes.

Broccoli and Rice Casserole
Terri Luckhurst

Gee Whiz! Cheese Whiz made good! Terri can't spend a lot of time in her kitchen so she likes quick and easy recipes when she does cook for her football star husband, Mick. Terri teamed up with her brother, Griff, for the Walker Cup, 1979 and the Curtis Cup, 1980.

½ **cup chopped celery**
½ **cup chopped onion**
½ **cup butter**
1 **10-ounce package frozen chopped broccoli,**
  cooked
2 **cups cooked rice**
1 **8-ounce jar Cheese Whiz**
1 **10¾-ounce can cream of mushroom soup**

Preheat oven to 350 degrees.
1. Cook celery and onion in butter until tender.
2. Add broccoli, rice, cheese and soup.
3. Mix well and spoon into greased 1½-quart baking dish.
4. Bake at 350 degrees for 45 minutes.

Cabbage Casserole   Fuzzy Zoeller

Fuzzy and his family live in New Albany, Indiana. A favorite
with the tournament galleries, he won the 1984 United
States Open at Winged Foot, Mamaroneck, Long Island,
with an 8-stroke play-off victory. Try this recipe when you
want to serve a special vegetable. It will soon be a family
favorite.

Yield: 8-12 servings

1 **head cabbage**
salt and pepper
1 **10¾-ounce can cream of celery soup**
2 **cups Velveeta cheese, cubed**
breadcrumbs or croutons
¼ **cup butter or margarine**

Preheat oven to 350 degrees.
1. Cut cabbage into pieces and cook until tender; add salt
   and pepper.
2. Place in greased casserole dish, pour soup over top.
   Distribute cheese over soup.
3. Sprinkle enough breadcrumbs to make a crispy topping.
4. Melt butter and pour over breadcrumbs.
5. Bake at 350 degrees for 30-40 minutes until brown on top.

Baked Corn on the Cob

Corn on the cob never had it so good! (See photograph)

Yield: 4 servings

4 ears sweet corn, husked
1/2 cup soft butter
1 tablespoon prepared mustard
1 teaspoon prepared horseradish
1 teaspoon salt
dash pepper

Preheat oven to 450 degrees.
1. Mix butter, mustard, horseradish, salt and pepper until light and fluffy.
2. Spread on corn and wrap in foil.
3. Bake in a 450-degree oven for 20-25 minutes.

Eggplant Italiano   Microwave

A classic.

Yield: 4-6 servings

1/2 large eggplant, peeled and sliced into 1/2-inch-thick slices
1 egg, beaten
3/4 cup Italian-seasoned breadcrumbs
1 8-ounce can tomato sauce
1/2 teaspoon Worcestershire sauce
1/2 teaspoon Italian seasonings
1 cup shredded Mozzarella cheese

1. Dip eggplant slices into egg and coat with breadcrumbs.
2. Preheat browning dish, uncovered, 5 minutes on High.
3. Place slices on preheated dish; microwave 3 minutes on High. Turn slices over and cook 2 to 3 minutes more.
4. Combine tomato sauce, Worcestershire sauce and seasonings. Pour over fried eggplant and top with cheese. Cover with glass lid.
5. Microwave on High 5 minutes until bubbly.

Stewed Eggplant

Nice 'n easy.

Yield: 6 servings

1 medium eggplant, peeled and sliced
1 large green pepper, sliced
2 medium onions, chopped
1/2 pound fresh mushrooms, sliced
2 tablespoons oil
1/2 6-ounce can tomato paste
1 tablespoon lemon juice
dash sugar and oregano
salt and pepper to taste

1. Sauté eggplant, green pepper, onions and mushrooms in oil.
2. Add remaining ingredients. Simmer until vegetables are tender. Do not overcook.

Mushroom-Artichoke
Casserole   Tom Kite

Tom first discovered golf at the age of six when his father
gave him a club. He has been swinging ever since. One of
the leading money winners, Tom enjoys doing golf-club
repairs when he's at home in Austin, Texas. Try this casserole when you serve a buffet-style meal.

Yield: 4-6 servings

3 cups sliced fresh mushrooms
½ cup chopped green onions with tops
4 tablespoons margarine
2 tablespoons flour
salt and pepper
¾ cup milk
1 teaspoon instant chicken bouillon
1 teaspoon lemon juice
⅛ teaspoon ground nutmeg
1 10-ounce package frozen artichoke hearts, cooked
   and drained
¾ cup breadcrumbs
1 tablespoon melted butter

Preheat oven to 350 degrees.
1. Cook mushrooms and green onions in the margarine till
   soft. Remove vegetables and set aside.
2. Blend flour, salt and a dash of pepper into the pan
   drippings. Add milk and bouillon, lemon juice and
   nutmeg. Cook and stir until bubbly. Add all vegetables
   and cook in skillet until brown.
3. Combine breadcrumbs with butter. Sprinkle around
   edge of 1-quart casserole. Bake at 350 degrees for 20
   minutes.

Potato Casserole

This is a cross between hash browns and scalloped potatoes.

Yield: 6 servings

3 medium russet potatoes (about 1 ½ pounds)
water
⅓ cup milk
3 tablespoons butter
2 eggs
1 ½ teaspoons salt
⅛ teaspoon pepper
1 large onion, chopped
paprika

Preheat oven to 375 degrees.
1. Peel and shred potatoes, about 4 cups. Immediately transfer potatoes to a bowl and cover with water to prevent discoloration. Set aside.
2. Remove ¼ cup water from potatoes and place in a small saucepan with milk and 2 tablespoons of butter; cook over medium heat to just under boiling. Remove and set aside.
3. Beat eggs with salt and pepper. Continue beating and slowly add the hot milk mixture; blend well.
4. Drain potatoes well by pouring into colander and pressing out the liquid.
5. Combine potatoes, onion and egg mixture. Rub the remaining 1 tablespoon of butter over sides and bottom of a 9 × 13-inch baking pan.
6. Spoon potato mixture into pan and sprinkle with paprika.
7. Bake uncovered in a 375-degree oven until set in center and edges are browned and crusty, about 50 minutes.
8. Cut into squares to serve.

 Did you ever try grating potatoes into ice water? Drain them just before using...they will be less starchy.

Fluffy Potato Casserole

These spuds are no duds!

Yield: 6-8 servings

2 cups hot or cold mashed potatoes
1 8-ounce package cream cheese, softened
1 small onion, finely chopped
2 eggs
2 tablespoons flour
salt and pepper to taste
1 3½-ounce can french-fried onions

Preheat oven to 300 degrees.
1. Put potatoes in large bowl of mixer.
2. Add cream cheese, onions, eggs, flour, salt and pepper. Beat at medium speed until well blended, then at high speed until light and fluffy.
3. Spoon into greased 9 × 9-inch baking dish.
4. Distribute fried onions evenly over top.
5. Bake uncovered in slow oven, 300 degrees, for 35 minutes.*

 If you prepare this ahead, add onions just before putting into oven.

*This recipe can be doubled using a 9 × 13-inch baking dish and baking for about 1 hour and 10 minutes. Cover with foil if onions start to get too brown.

Spinach Casserole   Dean Refram

Popeye never had it so good!! Barbara and Dean love this casserole. The artichokes add an interesting flavor that pleases everyone's palate. Serve with beef or veal. Dean won the 1975 Walt Disney World National Team Play (with Jim Colbert).

1 6-ounce can artichoke hearts, not marinated
¹/₂ cup chopped onions
¹/₄ cup margarine
2 10-ounce packages chopped frozen spinach, thawed
1 cup sour cream
¹/₂ cup grated Parmesan cheese

Preheat oven to 350 degrees.
1. Drain artichoke hearts; cut each heart into 6 sections.
2. Sauté onions in margarine until onions are soft, but not brown.
3. Combine all other ingredients.
4. Pour into greased square glass baking dish.
5. Bake at 350 degrees for 25 minutes.

Spinach Marliscin

Yield: 12 servings

¹/₂ cup butter or margarine, melted
10 eggs
¹/₂ cup unsifted all-purpose flour
1 teaspoon baking powder
1 teaspoon salt
1 10-ounce package frozen chopped spinach, thawed
1 8-ounce can green chilies, seeded and chopped
1 pint (2 cups) small-curd cottage cheese
¹/₂ pound Cheddar cheese, shredded
¹/₂ pound Monterey Jack cheese, shredded

Preheat oven to 400 degrees.
1. Place butter in 13 × 9 × 2-inch pan in warm oven, just to melt, about 3 minutes.
2. Beat eggs in a large bowl; mix in flour, baking powder and salt.
3. Squeeze thawed spinach very dry and add to egg mixture, along with melted butter, chilies and cheeses.
4. Pour mixture into pan and bake 15 minutes. Reduce heat to 350 degrees and bake an additional 35 to 40 minutes.
5. Let stand 5 minutes to set before serving.

Spinach Pie

Compatible with chicken or meat and certainly the palate!

Yield: 12 servings

1 bunch spinach, washed, trimmed and chopped
3 tablespoons olive oil
1 bunch green onions, finely chopped
¼ cup minced parsley
1 cup cottage cheese
1 cup feta cheese
4 eggs
½ teaspoon dill weed
1 cup flour
1 cup water
2 tablespoons butter or margarine, melted

Preheat oven to 350 degrees.
1. Squeeze all moisture from spinach. Heat 2 tablespoons oil in large skillet over medium heat. Add green onions and parsley and sauté until onions are softened.
2. Mix in spinach, cheeses, 2 lightly beaten eggs and dill weed.
3. Combine remaining 2 eggs, flour and water in medium bowl and mix well to make thin batter.
4. Coat 8 × 12-inch baking dish with remaining 1 tablespoon oil, and pour in half the batter, spreading evenly.
5. Top with spinach mixture and hot butter.
6. Pour remaining batter over.
7. Bake 45-50 minutes in a 350-degree oven until set. Cut into small squares. Serve immediately.

Squash Casserole Bruce Lietzke

Bruce is from Kansas City, Kansas, and now lives in Oklahoma with his wife, Rosemarie, and their young son. They like small gatherings and enjoy family life. This casserole is a wonderful accompaniment to any entrée and a sure winner.

2 tablespoons margarine
4 cups lightly boiled squash
1 medium onion, chopped
½ pound fresh mushrooms or 2 4-ounce cans
1 10¾-ounce can cream of mushroom soup
½ to ¾ cup shredded Cheddar cheese
1 egg
½ teaspoon salt (or to taste)
¼ to ½ cup breadcrumbs

Preheat oven to 350 degrees.
1. Melt margarine. Mash squash and add all other ingredients.
2. Stir well and salt to taste.
3. Pour into a greased 2-quart casserole.
4. Spread breadcrumbs on top.
5. Bake at 350 degrees for 35 minutes.

Party Squash   Microwave
Vance Heafner

A three-time All-American at North Carolina State, Vance is on his way to being one of the better players in the game.

Yield: 4-6 servings

5 medium to large yellow squash, sliced
4 medium onions, sliced
basil
thyme
grated Parmesan cheese

1. In a deep microwave casserole dish, place one layer of sliced squash, then a layer of sliced onion.
2. Sprinkle generously with basil, thyme and cheese.
3. Repeat sequence of layers, spices and cheese until dish is filled.
4. Cover, microwave on High for 15 minutes for vegetables that are slightly crunchy, 20 minutes for more tender vegetables.

Summer Squash Delight
Mark McCumber

"Summertime—and the living is easy," especially in Florida where Mark is busy designing golf courses as well as winning golf tournaments. He won the 1983 Western Open.

Yield: 6 servings

6-8 medium summer squash, sliced ¼-inch thick
2 large onions, sliced
½ cup butter
2 pieces Pepperidge Farm bread, toasted
½ cup grated Cheddar cheese
1 egg
½ cup canned evaporated milk
salt and pepper

Preheat oven to 350 degrees.
1. Sauté the squash and onion in butter.
2. Add the salt and pepper to taste. Break toasted bread into crumbs, saving some for top.
3. Add rest of bread and cheese to squash mixture.
4. Add slightly beaten egg. Toss gently to avoid breaking the tender squash. Pour milk over squash.
5. Pour into casserole dish and top with extra grated cheese and breadcrumbs.
6. Bake at 350 degrees for 30 minutes or until bubbly.

Sweet Potato Soufflé   Jim Jamieson

Flair without extravagance. You'll be nuts about this soufflé. Start a new tradition for your next Thanksgiving Day dinner. Jim and his family live in Atlantis, Florida.

Yield: 6 servings

1 29-ounce can sweet potatoes, drained of most of the juice
1 ¼ cups sugar
2 eggs
½ cup milk
½ teaspoon nutmeg
½ teaspoon cinnamon
¼ cup melted butter

Preheat oven to 350 degrees.
1. Blend all ingredients in mixer and pour into large greased casserole.
2. Bake at 350 degrees until firm, about 45 minutes.
3. Cover with topping and bake 10 minutes more.

Topping

½ cup brown sugar
¼ cup butter
½ cup chopped pecans

1. Melt the sugar and butter.
2. Spread on sweet potato mixture and sprinkle with the pecans.

Vegetable Casserole for Health Nuts   Mike Sullivan

Mike was born in Gary, Indiana and now lives in Ocala, Florida, with his wife, Sandy. They both like fresh, natural food and appreciate good health and fitness. This recipe is bursting with vitamins and minerals and is a joy to eat.

Yield: 2 servings

Cut up your pick of vegetables:
1 stem fresh broccoli
2 fresh carrots
1 fresh yellow squash
½ potato
10 small fresh mushrooms
½ zucchini
½ cup cauliflower
¼ cup frozen corn

1. Place vegetables on steamer in large pot with 1 inch of water and cover.
2. Turn on high; when water starts to steam, start timing.
3. For crisp vegetables, approximately 8 minutes. For softer vegetables, approximately 12 minutes. Spoon out vegetables onto plates and pour on sauce.

Sauce

⅓ cup butter
⅓ cup flour
1 cup milk
6 ounces cheese, cubed*
¼ teaspoon salt
⅛ teaspoon pepper
1 teaspoon parsley flakes, optional

1. Melt butter on medium heat; add flour, stirring until lumpy. Add 2 tablespoons milk, stir in 2 more tablespoons milk, stirring until smooth.

*We prefer Cheddar cheese with white flour and Monterey Jack cheese with whole wheat flour.

2. Add remaining milk, cheese, salt, pepper and parsley. Cook on medium heat, stirring until thick, about 10 minutes.

 This vegetable casserole is good with
1. Stuffed celery—use equal amounts of cream cheese and pimento-cheese spread mixed together.
2. Baked tomatoes—tomato halves sprinkled with buttered cracker crumbs and Parmesan cheese. Baked at 375 degrees for 20 minutes.
3. Your favorite muffins. It's also good served over egg noodles.

You can serve 8 people and cook most of the fresh vegetables at once, but allow more time for the cheese sauce. The more milk in the pan, the longer it takes to thicken.

Baked Stuffed Tomatoes

Yield: 6 servings

6 medium tomatoes
4 tablespoons finely chopped green pepper
2 tablespoons finely chopped onions
¼ teaspoon sugar
dash oregano
salt and pepper
4 tablespoons melted butter or margarine
¾ cup fine dry breadcrumbs

Preheat oven to 375 degrees.
1. Cut off tops of tomatoes, scoop out centers. Chop pulp. Mix with green pepper, onion, sugar, oregano, salt, pepper. Mix breadcrumbs with butter and add ¼ of this mixture to vegetables.
2. Spoon into tomato shells.
3. Spoon remaining breadcrumb mixture over tops of stuffed tomatoes.
4. Bake uncovered at 375 degrees for 25 minutes or until tomatoes are tender and breadcrumbs are lightly brown and crisp.

Nutmeal Zucchini   Microwave

An interesting variation.

Yield: 2 servings

2 large zucchini
2 thick slices bread, crusts removed
6 tablespoons milk
2 teaspoons margarine or butter
4 tablespoons finely chopped walnuts
4 tablespoons grated cheese
1 egg
1 tablespoon finely chopped parsley

1. Cut the zucchini in half lengthwise.
2. Place bread in bowl, pouring milk over and leave until milk is absorbed.
3. Mash the bread; stir in margarine, nuts, cheese and egg to form soft stuffing.
4. Pile the stuffing on top of the zucchini. Arrange them close together in a dish that fits them snugly.
5. Microwave on High for 4-5 minutes until tender. Sprinkle with chopped parsley.

Zucchini Medley   Steve Menchinella

Steve is the golf professional at Sunnyside Country Club in Fresno, California. This recipe is one of his and his wife, Peggy's, favorites.

Yield: 4 servings

1 pound small zucchini
1/2 onion, chopped
1 8-ounce can tomato sauce
1/2 teaspoon sugar
1 clove garlic, pressed
1/2 teaspoon salt
1/4 teaspoon oregano
2 tablespoons vegetable oil
4-6 tablespoons grated Romano cheese

1. Scrub zucchini; slice 1/4-inch thick.
2. Mix onions and zucchini in a greased 1 1/2-quart casserole.
3. Combine tomato sauce with sugar, garlic, salt, oregano and vegetable oil. Pour over the zucchini. Sprinkle with cheese.
4. Cook, covered, 7 minutes. Stir for a minute. Cook 6-7 minutes longer. Let stand 5 minutes before serving.

 Delicious served with shrimp.

Stuffed Peppers Creole   Low Fat

A family favorite.

Yield: 4 servings (140 calories each)

4 large green peppers
1/2 pound bite-sized shrimp, cooked and cleaned
1 medium onion, minced
1/2 cup cooked rice
salt and pepper to taste
1 6-ounce can tomato paste
6 ounces water

Preheat oven to 350 degrees.
1. Wash peppers. Remove tops, seeds, and pulp.
2. Immerse peppers in boiling water and cook 3 minutes. Remove and place in lightly greased casserole.
3. Combine shrimp, onion, rice, salt and pepper; mix well.
4. Fill peppers with mixture. Cover and bake in a 350-degree oven for 20 minutes.
5. Remove from oven; combine tomato paste and water and pour over peppers.
6. Return to oven and bake 5 minutes longer.

OOOOOOOOOOOOOOOOOO

Accompaniments

OOOOOOOOOOOOOOOOOO

Sugared Bacon Strips
Arnold Palmer

Arnold Palmer has had a most distinguished career as an athlete and businessman. "Arnie's Army" has followed him whenever he plays, always faithful to their leader. Winnie and Arnold live in Latrobe, Pennsylvania, and enjoy this different dish. Make enough to feed Arnie's Army!

Yield: 4 servings

½ pound to 1 pound bacon, at room temperature
1 cup brown sugar

Preheat oven to 275 degrees.
1. Roll (or pat or shake) raw bacon in brown sugar and place strips on any flat pan with sides.
2. Bake in slow oven (275 degrees) for about 25-30 minutes until dark brown.
3. You may turn over once with tongs. When bacon appears well done, remove with tongs and drain on paper toweling.
4. As it cools, it will get hard and can then be broken into smaller pieces or served whole.
5. This tedious chore can be done earlier in the day and the bacon stored in aluminum foil. Reheat to serve.

Spiced Cranberries

Try this for a new twist.

Yield: 2 cups

1 pound fresh cranberries
2 cups sugar
1 cup water
5 whole cloves
2 teaspoons allspice
2 3-inch cinnamon sticks

1. Wash berries, remove stems, drain.
2. In a large saucepan, combine sugar and water and bring to a boil over medium heat. Stir constantly until sugar dissolves.
3. Add cloves, allspice, cinnamon; reduce heat and simmer 5 minutes.
4. Add cranberries and stir once or twice until berries start to pop, about 3 minutes.
5. Remove from heat and cool. Pour into a 1-quart jar and refrigerate, covered, for several days before serving. Keeps indefinitely.

Hot Fruit Compote

A good side dish with meat or poultry. Also great over vanilla ice cream.

Yield: 6-8 servings

1 16-ounce can peach slices, drained very well
1 16-ounce can pineapple chunks, drained very well
1 11-ounce can mandarin oranges, drained very well
1 21-ounce can cherry pie filling
2 tablespoons dry Tang

Preheat oven to 325 degrees.
1. Put first three ingredients into a greased casserole.
2. Pour cherry pie filling over and add Tang; mix gently.
3. Heat in a 325-degree oven, covered, for 20 minutes.
Variations: 1 box dried apricots and/or 1 box dried pitted
   prunes which have been plumped in water.

Seven Fruit Jam

A layer for every day of the week.

Yield: 1 gallon

strawberries
boysenberries
cherries
plums
apricots
raspberries
grapes

1. As each fruit comes into season, cook 2 cups of sugar
   with 2 cups of the fruit. Boil hard for 10 minutes.
2. Test with candy thermometer as for any jam; or put
   spoonful in deep freeze until cool; should set tightly,
   not stiff.
3. Keep gallon jar in refrigerator until you have 7 layers;
   stir all together and enjoy.

Green Pepper Jelly Microwave

Yield: 6 cups

**¼ cup seeded and chopped hot green pepper
(Anaheim or jalapeño)**
¾ cup seeded and finely chopped green bell pepper
6½ cups sugar
1½ cups apple cider vinegar
6 ounces Certo liquid fruit pectin
2-3 drops green food coloring

1. Mix peppers and juices with sugar and vinegar in 5-quart casserole.
2. Cover and microwave on High for 10-12 minutes, stirring once. Let stand 5 minutes.
3. Add liquid fruit pectin and food coloring. Stir well.
4. Pour into hot, sterilized jars, seal with lids and store in refrigerator.

 Speaking of jelly, if you lightly spread a thin coat of any jelly over hamburgers or roast before cooking, people will swear you've got a charcoal grill right in your kitchen.

Sherri's Perfect Kosher Pickles

Better than store bought. Do this with friends and enjoy!

Yield: 24 quarts

3 pecks pickling cucumbers
24 quart jars, sterilized
dill weed
1¾ cups salt (kosher)
12 teaspoons pickling spice
24 bay leaves
48 cloves garlic, peeled
24 red peppers

1. Wash and scrub the cucumbers.
2. Sterilize the jars in the dishwasher. Boil the caps.
3. Put a piece of dill on the bottom of each jar. Stuff each jar with the cucumbers.
4. Add to each jar 1 heaping tablespoon salt, ½ teaspoon pickling spice, 1 bay leaf, 2 cloves garlic, 1 red pepper. Place a piece of dill on top. Fill each jar with cold tap water. Shake to mix, seal. Be sure the cucumbers are covered with the water.

 Pickling process takes from 7 days to 10 days, depending on the weather.

Rice and Onion Soup Casserole

Tastes like wild rice. Great with chicken or lamb.

Yield: 2 servings

½ cup long-grain rice
1 cup chicken broth
½ package Lipton's Onion Soup Mix
1 4½-ounce jar button mushrooms

Preheat oven to 350 degrees.
1. Mix all ingredients together.
2. Bake 50 minutes at 350 degrees, uncovered, and 10 minutes, covered.

Rivvles   Patrick Lindsey

The 1983 British Columbia Open winner, Pat now lives in Florida. His special interests include hunting and reading. Serve this instead of noodles with beef. Note from Patrick: "This is an old Lindsey family recipe. Basically, rivvles are just beef noodles that some Lindsey somewhere was too lazy to roll."

Yield: 4 servings

broth from a pot roast, or canned beef broth
3 or 4 eggs
2 to 3 cups flour

1. Take the broth from a pot roast that you've been cooking. If you do not have that, canned beef broth will work.
2. Crack eggs into a mixing bowl.
3. Add flour to the eggs, enough that after you have beaten it with a fork, little balls of dough can be formed.
4. Bring the broth to a boil, slowly drop in the small balls of dough and cook until they are firm (approximately 12-15 minutes).

Sauce Bordelaise

Superb over broiled steak or roast beef.

Yield: 6-8 servings

1 tablespoon chopped shallots
1 cup red wine
1 cup commercial demi-glacé (or deglazed pan
**   drippings)**
1 tablespoon butter
1 tablespoon chopped parsley

1. Add chopped shallots to red wine and boil gently until reduced to ⅓ cup.
2. Add demi-glacé and return to a simmer. Remove from heat.
3. Whisk in butter. Strain.
4. Add chopped parsley and serve.

Hollandaise Sauce Microwave

Irresistible!

Yield: 1½ cups

¼ cup butter or margarine
¼ cup light cream
2 egg yolks
1 tablespoon lemon juice
½ teaspoon dry mustard
½ teaspoon salt
dash hot pepper sauce

1. Melt butter in medium bowl on High for 1 minute.
2. Stir in remaining ingredients. Microwave on High for 1 minute, stirring every 15 seconds.
3. Stir briskly with a wire whisk until light and fluffy.

 Serve with fish or vegetables.

Lemon Tahini Sauce

Try this . . . you'll love it!

Yield: About 5 cups

1 ¹/₂ cups buttermilk
¹/₂ cup lemon juice
¹/₂ cup tamari (soy sauce)
³/₄ cup safflower oil
2 scallions, chopped
¹/₂ clove garlic, chopped
¹/₄ onion, finely chopped
1 ¹/₂ stalks celery, chopped
¹/₂ cup minced fresh parsley leaves
¹/₄ cup chopped green pepper
¹/₄ cup peeled, seeded, and chopped cucumber
salt and pepper
1 cup unsalted tahini (sesame seed paste)

1. In a blender, blend ingredients down to and including cucumber. Add a pinch of salt and pepper.
2. Add the tahini and blend the mixture until it is thick and well combined.

  Serve the sauce with vegetables.

Bob Hope's Favorite Mint Sauce   Bob Hope

You can bank on this!

Yield: 2 cups

1 bunch fresh mint
³/₄ cup white wine vinegar
¹/₄ cup lemon juice
¹/₄ cup water
¹/₂ cup honey
¹/₂ teaspoon salt
dash of Worcestershire sauce
¹/₂ cup green mint jelly

1. Cut or chop mint very fine and combine with other ingredients.
2. Let steep for several hours.

 Great with roast lamb!

Hot Fudge Sauce   Jim Simons

Jim Simons, from Pittsburgh, Pennsylvania, now lives with his wife and family in Tequesta, Florida. Jim started playing golf when he was nine, and won the 1982 Crosby Pro-Am. He is active in the brokerage business as an investment executive.

Yield: 1 quart

½ cup cocoa
1 cup sugar
1 cup light corn syrup
½ cup evaporated milk
¼ teaspoon salt
3 tablespoons salted butter
1 teaspoon vanilla extract

1. Combine all the ingredients except vanilla.
2. Cook over medium heat, stirring constantly, until the mixture comes to a full boil. Boil for 3 minutes, stirring occasionally.
3. Remove mixture from heat; add vanilla.
4. Store in quart jar in refrigerator until needed.

 Warm in microwave or on stove before using.

Orange Cranberry Sauce

A great way to dress up the holiday bird.

Yield: 3 cups

1 cup sugar
¹/₂ cup fresh orange juice
¹/₂ cup water
3 cups fresh cranberries, rinsed and stemmed
2 tablespoons cognac
1 tablespoon grated orange peel
1 tablespoon lemon juice

1. Combine sugar, orange juice and water in large saucepan and bring to a boil, stirring, until sugar is dissolved.
2. Add berries and cook until popped, about 5 minutes.
3. Mash some of the berries. Cool 5 minutes.
4. Blend in remaining ingredients. Cool completely.
5. Refrigerate sauce until ready to serve.

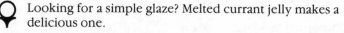 Looking for a simple glaze? Melted currant jelly makes a delicious one.

Quick and Easy Pizza Sauce
Microwave

Yield: 1 cup

1 6-ounce can tomato sauce
¹/₂ cup water
2 teaspoons instant minced onion
2 teaspoons sugar
¹/₂ teaspoon salt
¹/₄ teaspoon oregano
¹/₄ teaspoon basil
¹/₄ teaspoon garlic powder
¹/₈ teaspoon pepper

1. Combine all ingredients in bowl.
2. Microwave on High for 2 to 4 minutes or until mixture boils.

 Add favorite toppings: mushrooms, onion, olives, anchovies, etc.

San Francisco Turkey Stuffing

A Bay Area classic.

Yield: Enough for a 16-20 pound turkey

2 large onions, chopped
4 stalks celery, chopped
1 turkey liver, chopped
4 tablespoons butter
½ cup red wine
2 10-ounce packages frozen spinach
2 loaves day-old sourdough French bread
water
1 tablespoon poultry seasoning
1 tablespoon sage
1½ tablespoons salt
¼ teaspoon pepper
3 eggs, beaten

1. Brown onions, celery and liver in butter.
2. Add wine and simmer 20 minutes. Meanwhile, cook spinach until tender. Drain well and chop.
3. Remove crusts from bread, cut into 1-inch cubes; moisten slightly with water and squeeze dry.
4. Add vegetable-wine mixture and spinach to bread; add seasonings and mix lightly.
5. Stir in beaten eggs. If necessary, moisten with more wine. Stuff into turkey gently.

Chili Sauce Low Fat

It does the job!

Yield: 3-4 cups (6 calories per tablespoon)

5 medium tomatoes
1 green pepper
1 onion
1/2 cup vinegar
1 teaspoon sugar
1 teaspoon salt
1/2 teaspoon chili powder
1/4 teaspoon finely chopped chives
1/2 teaspoon cinnamon
pinch of cayenne
pinch of ginger

1. Wash tomatoes and cut into small pieces. Wash pepper, remove seeds and white pulp, cut in small pieces.
2. Peel and chop onion and combine with remaining ingredients in pot. Bring to a boil.
3. Cook over low heat until thick, stirring several times.
4. Pour thickened mixture immediately into hot sterilized jars.
5. Seal and store.

6th Hole, Pebble Beach Golf Links

7th Hole, Pebble Beach Golf Links

8th Hole, Pebble Beach Golf Links

12th Hole, Spyglass Hill Golf Course

16th Hole, Cypress Point Golf Course

15th Hole, Cypress Point Golf Course

16th Hole, Spyglass Hill Golf Course

17th Hole, Cypress Point Golf Course

Desserts

Apple Casserole   Terri Luckhurst

"Five foot two, eyes of blue," Terri is a southern gal with lots of skill on the course and in the kitchen. This dessert is an easy version of an old favorite.

Yield: 6-8 servings

¾ cup butter at room temperature
12 ounces Velveeta cheese
1 ½ cups sugar
1 cup flour
2 20-ounce cans sliced apples

Preheat oven to 375 degrees.
1. Cream softened butter and cheese in a mixer. Add sugar and flour and set aside.
2. Butter a shallow casserole dish.
3. Pour in apples and spread around. Cover apples with the cheese mixture.
4. Bake at 375 degrees for 30 minutes.

Apple Crisp   Doug Tewell

Doug started golf at the age of 12 in Baton Rouge, Louisiana, and turned professional in 1971. This recipe is a good old standby with the Tewell family. You can't miss with the combination of apples, cinnamon and cake. A perfect ending to any meal.

Yield: 6 servings

4 cups peeled and sliced apples
1 teaspoon cinnamon
½ teaspoon salt
¼ cup water
¾ cup flour
1 cup sugar
⅓ cup margarine

Preheat oven to 350 degrees.
1. Place the apples in a buttered 10 × 6-inch or similar baking dish.
2. Sprinkle with cinnamon, salt and water.
3. Mix together the flour, sugar and margarine.
4. Drop this mixture over apples.
5. Bake 40 minutes at 350 degrees.

 To keep fresh apples, pears and peaches from turning brown, put them in cold water to which a little lemon juice has been added.

Almond Pound Cake   Joey Rassett

Joey and his wife, Drew, live in Scottsdale, Arizona, and look forward to many rewarding years in golf. Joey was low amateur in the 1981 United States Open and joined the tour in 1983. Their favorite pound cake is not too sweet, yet a treat for all.

Yield: 1 cake

4 eggs
a bit of milk
2 cups flour
2 cups sugar
1 teaspoon baking powder
¹/₄ teaspoon salt
1 cup vegetable shortening or ¹/₂ margarine
**   and ¹/₂ shortening**
1 ¹/₂ teaspoons almond extract
³/₄ cup milk

Preheat oven to 325 degrees.
1. Break eggs into measuring cup; fill to 1 cup mark with milk.
2. In a mixing bowl, combine the egg-milk mixture, flour, sugar, baking powder, salt, shortening and almond extract.
3. Beat at medium speed with electric mixer for 3 minutes, using a rubber spatula to scrape the batter away from the sides of the bowl.
4. Add additional ³/₄ cup of milk and beat a minute or so more. (It may be easier to hand mix at this point.)
5. Pour into greased and floured tube cake pan. Bake at 325 degrees for approximately 1 hour or until toothpick inserted comes out clean.
6. Cool on wire rack for 30 minutes.

 Be sure to keep the baking powder dry, lest it lose its leavening.

Blueberry Banana Delight
Dean Refram

A very appealing dessert that only takes a few minutes to assemble and looks like a work of art. Barbara and Dean love to indulge in this fruited paradise whenever possible. They are true southerners, having been born and bred in Florida.

Yield: 1 9 × 13-inch panful

Crust

¼ cup margarine or butter
1 cup flour
½ cup chopped pecans

Preheat oven to 350 degrees.
1. Mix the ingredients together.
2. Press in bottom of a 9 × 13-inch pan and bake at 350 degrees for 15-20 minutes.
3. Cool thoroughly.

Filling

1 8-ounce package cream cheese, softened
1 cup powdered sugar
1 large carton Cool Whip topping
2 large bananas
1½ pints fresh blueberries*

1. Mix the cream cheese with sugar.
2. Add mixture to one cup Cool Whip. Spread on crust and refrigerate for one hour.
3. Slice bananas on top of cream-cheese mixture and then add blueberries on top.
4. Top with remainder of Cool Whip topping.

*Can also be made with blueberry pie filling.

Connecticut Blueberry Cake
Greg Powers

Greg is a real sports fan, following all the sporting events. He lives in Florida, but admits you don't have to be a Yankee to love this cake. A delightful dessert, especially with fresh blueberries—everyone will want seconds.

Yield: 1 9 × 9-inch cake

¼ cup butter or margarine
¾ cup sugar
1 egg
2 cups flour
2 teaspoons baking powder
½ teaspoon salt
½ cup milk
2 cups fresh blueberries

Preheat oven to 375 degrees.
1. Cream butter; beat in sugar, add egg and beat well.
2. Add sifted dry ingredients alternately with milk, beating until smooth.
3. Fold in berries.
4. Pour into a 9 × 9-inch pan; sprinkle with topping.
5. Bake at 375 degrees about 35 minutes.

Topping

¼ cup butter
½ teaspoon cinnamon
⅓ cup sugar
⅓ cup flour

Cut butter into dry ingredients until texture is crumblike.

Carrot Cake   Peter Jacobsen

A winner! Peter is a happy, personable young man who delights sponsors and galleries at every stop on tour. He has a special interest in music and is very comfortable performing in front of people.

Yield: 1 9 × 13-inch cake

4 eggs
2 cups sugar
1¼ cups Wesson oil
2 cups flour
2 teaspoons soda
3 teaspoons cinnamon
1 teaspoon salt
3 cups grated raw carrots
1 8-ounce can crushed pineapple, drained

Preheat oven to 350 degrees.
1. Beat eggs, add sugar and oil.
2. Sift flour, soda, cinnamon and salt. Add to egg mixture.
3. Add raw carrots and pineapple last.
4. Pour into greased and floured 9 × 13-inch pan.
5. Bake at 350 degrees for 35 minutes; top with cream cheese icing.

Cream Cheese Icing

½ cup butter, softened
1 8-ounce package cream cheese, softened
1 box powdered sugar
1 cup chopped pecans
1 teaspoon vanilla extract

1. Blend butter and cheese; add sugar, nuts and vanilla.
2. Spread while cake is slightly warm.

Easy Cheesecake   Allen Miller

Allen established an outstanding record as an amateur and is now ready for big wins as a professional. He is married to Cindy Kessler, formerly of the LPGA tour and they live in Pensacola, Florida, with their daughter, Kelly.

Yield: 8 servings

3 large eggs
2 8-ounce packages cream cheese, softened
²/₃ cup sugar
1 teaspoon vanilla extract
1 unbaked 9-inch graham cracker pie crust
cinnamon

Preheat oven to 350 degrees.
1. Blend ingredients until smooth and pour into pie crust. Sprinkle with cinnamon.
2. Bake at 350 degrees for 45 minutes or until done.
3. Cool thoroughly.

Topping

1 8-ounce container sour cream
2 tablespoons sugar
1 teaspoon vanilla extract

Preheat oven to 400 degrees.
1. Mix the sour cream with the sugar and vanilla.
2. Spread over top. Bake at 400 degrees for 5 minutes.

Dana's Refrigerator Cheesecake   Dana Booth

Dana is very busy running the Pro Shop at Spyglass Hill Golf Course, Pebble Beach. He doesn't have much time to cook, but enjoys this cheesecake whenever he can.

Yield: 1 9-inch cake

1 8-ounce package cream cheese, softened
1 cup sugar
¼ teaspoon salt
1 teaspoon vanilla extract
3 egg yolks
3 egg whites
½ pint whipping cream
1 prepared 9-inch graham cracker pie crust

1. Beat thoroughly the cream cheese, sugar, salt, vanilla and egg yolks.
2. Beat the egg whites and whipping cream separately.
3. Gently fold the egg whites and whipped cream into the cream cheese mixture.
4. Pour mixture into the pie shell.
5. Place in refrigerator overnight.

Cherry Jamboree   Mike Reid

One of the most important steps to success for Mike was his marriage to Randolyn. Now the Reid family is working together. When off the tour, the Reids love to ski in Utah. This dessert is special and can be done ahead.

Yield: 1 9 × 9-inch panful

**2 lemons, juiced or 4 tablespoons frozen 100%
    lemon juice
2 egg yolks, beaten
½ teaspoon mustard
¼ teaspoon salt
30 marshmallows
1 8-ounce can pineapple chunks, drained
1 8-ounce bottle red maraschino cherries
1 cup pecans
½ pint whipping cream, whipped**

1. Cook lemon juice, egg yolks, mustard and salt in a double boiler until thick.
2. To this, add 30 marshmallows and stir until dissolved.
3. Pour into a greased 9-inch square pan or casserole dish. Let cool.
4. Add pineapple chunks, cherries and pecans; then stir in whipped cream.
5. Let stand in refrigerator overnight.

Topping

**4 egg yolks
1 tablespoon mild vinegar
15 marshmallows
1 cup whipping cream, whipped**

1. In a double boiler, cook egg yolks, vinegar and marsh-mallows until marshmallows are melted. Let cool.
2. Add whipped cream. Spread on dessert.

Sweet Chocolate Cake   Sally Dodge

Promise her anything, but give her chocolate! Sally is from Virginia but now lives in Carmel, California. She has become known as one of the best teaching professionals on the Monterey Peninsula, working at Pebble Beach Golf Links.

Yield: 1 2-layer 9-inch cake

4 ounces sweet chocolate
½ cup boiling water
1 cup butter or margarine
2 cups sugar
4 egg yolks
1 teaspoon vanilla extract
2¼ cups sifted all-purpose flour
1 teaspoon baking soda
½ teaspoon salt
1 cup buttermilk
4 egg whites, stiffly beaten

Preheat oven to 350 degrees.
1. Melt chocolate in boiling water. Cool; cream butter and sugar until fluffy.
2. Add yolks, one at a time, beating well after each.
3. Blend in vanilla and chocolate. Sift flour with soda and salt.
4. Add flour mixture alternately with buttermilk to chocolate mixture, beating after each addition until smooth. Fold in beaten whites.
5. Pour into 2 9-inch layer pans, greased and lined on bottoms with paper.
6. Bake at 350 degrees for 30-35 minutes. Cool before frosting.

 Grease and flour only the bottom of layer cake pans. The cake will climb higher and evener if the pan sides are untouched.

"Texas" Chocolate Sheet Cake
Loren Roberts

We call this a "Texas" Chocolate Sheet Cake because, made in a jelly roll pan, it looks as if it can feed the entire state! Loren and his wife, Kim, live in California and know that wherever you live, you will enjoy this cake.

Yield: A lot of cake!

2 cups flour
2 cups sugar
1 cup butter
2 ½ tablespoons cocoa
1 cup water
2 eggs
½ cup milk or buttermilk
1 tablespoon baking soda
1 teaspoon vanilla extract

Preheat oven to 400 degrees.
1. Mix together flour and sugar in large bowl.
2. Melt butter and combine with cocoa and water; add this to flour and sugar mixture.
3. Beat eggs and milk and add baking soda and vanilla.
4. Mix all together and bake in greased jelly roll pan for about 30 minutes. Ice while hot.

Icing

½ cup butter
2 ½ tablespoons cocoa
4 tablespoons milk
1 box powdered sugar
1 teaspoon vanilla extract

1. Melt butter; add cocoa, milk and powdered sugar.
2. Stir on low heat until all sugar is melted and smooth. Add vanilla and pour over hot cake.

Tom's Favorite Chocolate Cake   Tom Purtzer

This cake is super moist and doesn't last long in the Purtzer household. Tom, who has one of the better overall records on the tour, lives with his family in Phoenix, Arizona.

Yield: 1 9 × 13-inch cake

2 cups sugar
½ cup unsweetened cocoa
2 cups flour
pinch of salt
½ cup shortening, melted
2 teaspoons baking soda
2 cups boiling water
2 eggs
1 teaspoon vanilla extract

Preheat oven to 350 degrees.
1. Mix sugar, cocoa, flour, and salt together.
2. Make hole in center and add shortening in middle.
3. Mix baking soda into water; it will bubble. Pour over shortening; stir everything well.
4. Spoon into a greased 9 × 13-inch pan.
5. Bake at 350 degrees approximately 30-40 minutes.
6. Frost with your favorite frosting.

 To measure shortening, use a cup that will hold twice as much as you need; fill the cup half full of water, add shortening till water reaches the top.

Chocolate Cheesecake   Andy North

A pro recipe! Andy, the 1978 United States Open winner, is interested in all sports, but next to golf, football is Number One. For special occasions at home with his family, Andy loves this cheesecake—a real delicacy.

Yield: 1 9-inch cake

Crust

1 box chocolate wafer crumbs (1 ¼ cups)
½ stick butter, melted
2 tablespoons brown sugar

Combine ingredients, press into a greased 9-inch springform pan.

Filling

⅓ cup flour
¼ teaspoon baking soda (scant)
8 ounces sweet chocolate
3 large eggs
¾ cup sugar
8 ounces cream cheese, softened
1 ¼ cups heavy cream, unwhipped
¼ teaspoon vanilla extract

Preheat oven to 325 degrees.
1. Sift flour and baking soda. Set aside.
2. Melt chocolate, remove from heat and cool slightly.
3. In a small bowl, beat eggs until thick. Beat in sugar, one tablespoon at a time, until mixture is thick and ivory colored.
4. Without washing beater, beat cream cheese until fluffy in large bowl; add cream and vanilla, beating until smooth and of whipping cream consistency.
5. Add chocolate, beating gently to blend. With spatula, fold in egg mixture, then fold in flour mixture.
6. Bake 1 ½ hours at 325 degrees.
7. Cool; top will crack. Cover with topping and chill. Serve at room temperature.

Topping

1 tablespoon powdered sugar, sifted
5 teaspoons crème de cacao
¾ cup whipping cream

Whip cream, sugar and crème de cacao. Spread over cheesecake.

Chocolate Chip Cake

John Geertsen, Sr.

John Geertsen, Sr., one of the finest teaching professionals, will tell you that this recipe will soon be among your all-time favorites. Who can resist a piece of chocolate chip cake and a glass of milk?

Yield: 1 9 × 13-inch cake

1 teaspoon soda
1 cup dates, chopped
1 cup hot water
1 cup sugar
1 cup butter
1 ¾ cups flour
2 eggs
1 tablespoon cocoa
1 teaspoon vanilla extract
1 cup chocolate chips
½ cup nuts, chopped

Preheat oven to 350 degrees.
1. Add soda to dates and pour hot water over; allow to sit.
2. Cream sugar and butter; combine with dates, flour, eggs, cocoa and vanilla.
3. Add ½ cup chocolate chips.
4. Pour into greased 9 × 13-inch pan. Sprinkle rest of chocolate chips and nuts on top. Bake at 350 degrees for 40 minutes.

Chocolate Ice Box Dessert

President and Mrs. Gerald R. Ford

A favorite from the Oval Office.

Yield: 1 9 × 9-inch cake

angel food cake *
6 eggs
1 12-ounce package chocolate chips
4 tablespoons sugar
6 tablespoons water
2 teaspoons vanilla extract
1 teaspoon salt
2 cups whipping cream

1. Line a 9 × 9-inch pan with waxed paper. Slice angel food cake and place a layer of cake in pan.
2. Separate eggs; beat egg yolks.
3. Melt chocolate chips in a double boiler over water; add sugar and water, mix well, being sure sugar melts.
4. Remove from heat and stir the hot chocolate mixture gradually into the beaten egg yolks; beat until smooth.
5. Cool chocolate mixture. Add vanilla and salt; mix.
6. Beat the egg whites until stiff; whip cream. Fold egg whites into the cooled chocolate mixture and then fold in whipped cream.
7. Place a layer of the chocolate mixture on the sliced cake, then another layer of cake, then a layer of chocolate.
8. Place in refrigerator and chill overnight.
   This may be frozen and used later. Be sure to chill overnight before freezing.

   *Angel food cake slices better when frozen.

Nell's Chocolate Pie
Lanny Wadkins

When Lanny attacks a golf course, watch out! He is a bold, calculating player who gives a spectacular performance whenever he plays. Lanny and his wife, Penelope, don't count calories when they have this dessert.

Yield: 1 9-inch pie

1 cup sugar
2 tablespoons cocoa
4 tablespoons flour
dash of salt
2 cups milk, heated
3 egg yolks
2 tablespoons butter
1 teaspoon vanilla extract
baked pie shell

1. Mix thoroughly all dry ingredients.
2. Add milk and cook over low heat, stirring constantly. When mixture starts to boil, cook for only 1 minute longer and remove from heat.
3. Beat the egg yolks, then add half of the heated mixture to the beaten yolks and mix well.
4. Add remaining half of the mixture along with the butter and vanilla.
5. Stir well and pour into a pie shell.

Meringue

3 egg whites
3 tablespoons sugar
1 teaspoon vanilla extract

Preheat oven to 350 degrees.
1. Beat egg whites until stiff. Add sugar and vanilla.
2. Spoon on top of pie and bake at 350 degrees for 5 or 10 minutes. Do not let it burn!

Pie Pastry

3 cups flour
1 cup shortening
1 teaspoon salt
1 beaten egg
1 tablespoon vinegar
5 tablespoons ice water

Preheat oven to 400 degrees.
1. Sift flour and mash together the flour, salt and shortening before adding other ingredients.
2. Bake at 400 degrees for 20 minutes. Will make 3 pie shells.
3. Store in refrigerator or freeze until ready to use.

Chocolate Chess Pie

Dudley Wysong, Jr.

This pie says "Check Mate." What a sweet treat after a round of golf. More than enough for two foursomes. Dudley is the 1966 Phoenix Open winner.

Yield: 2 9-inch pies

1 ³/₄ cups sugar
¹/₃ cup cocoa
1 ¹/₄ cups margarine, melted
4 eggs, beaten
¹/₄ cup evaporated milk
1 teaspoon vanilla extract
2 unbaked 9-inch pie shells
Cool Whip topping (optional)

Preheat oven to 350 degrees.
1. Combine sugar, cocoa, and margarine. Mix well.
2. Add eggs, milk, vanilla; mix thoroughly. Pour into pie shells and bake at 350 degrees for 35-40 minutes.
3. Cool. Serve with Cool Whip topping, if desired.

Billy's Scrumptious Cream Pie
Billy Casper

Billy Casper was the second man to pass the Million Dollar Mark in tour earnings. Since joining the tour in 1955, he has won almost every tournament. His special interests now center on his family and church work, and he plays on the senior tour.

Yield: 2 8-inch pies

28 ounces cream cheese, softened
3 cups whipping cream (heaviest)
1 1/2 cups powdered sugar
1 1/2 teaspoons vanilla extract
2 8-inch chocolate or graham cracker crusts

1. Mix cream cheese and whipping cream at low speed until smooth.
2. Add powdered sugar and vanilla. Mix at low speed until smooth, then whip at high speed until it is set up.
3. Pour into pie crusts and refrigerate for 3-4 hours.
4. Add berry toppings, caramel or fudge at last minute, if desired.

Derby Pie   Curtis Strange

Curtis Strange is one of the more determined and talented players and thus, one of the most successful men in the business. Curtis and his wife, Sarah, enjoy this dessert, a combination of nuts and chocolate chips topped with ice cream.

Yield: 1 9-inch pie

1 cup sugar
½ cup flour
2 eggs, slightly beaten
½ cup butter, melted
1 cup pecans (or walnuts)
1 cup chocolate chips
1 teaspoon vanilla extract
1 unbaked 9-inch pie shell

Preheat oven to 350 degrees.
1. Mix sugar and flour. Add slightly beaten eggs and cooled, melted butter.
2. Add pecans, chocolate chips and vanilla.
3. Pour into an unbaked pie shell and bake 45 minutes at 350 degrees.* Serve warm with ice cream.

*Best if slightly underbaked.

Five-Layered Dessert   Larry Hinson

We call this a Par 5 Delight. It's a colorful layered dessert that's a delight to the eye as well as the taste buds. Larry and his family live in Douglas, Georgia.

Yield: 1 9 × 13-inch panful

First Layer

1 cup flour
1/2 cup butter
1/2 cup chopped nuts

Preheat oven to 350 degrees.
Mix all ingredients together. Press into a 9 × 13-inch baking pan. Bake 15 minutes at 350 degrees until light brown.

Second Layer

1 8-ounce package cream cheese, softened
1 cup powdered sugar
1 3/4 cups Cool Whip topping

Mix and spread over cooled first layer.

Third Layer

2 3-ounce packages vanilla instant-pudding mix
3 cups milk

Mix together until it starts to set and pour over second layer.

Fourth Layer

Cover with Cool Whip topping.

Fifth Layer

Cover with cherry or blueberry pie filling.

Triple Fudge Cake   Doug Tewell

Fudge, fudge and more fudge! A nutty chocolate favorite with Pam and Doug. You will get rave notices when you serve it.

Yield: 1 9 × 13-inch cake

1 4½-ounce package chocolate pudding
1 18½-ounce package Devil's Food Cake Mix (dry)
1 6-ounce package semi-sweet chocolate chips
½ cup chopped nuts

Preheat oven to 350 degrees.
1. Grease and flour a 9 × 13-inch pan.
2. Cook chocolate pudding according to package directions.
3. Blend dry cake mix into hot pudding. Pour into pan.
4. Sprinkle top of batter with chocolate chips and chopped nuts.
5. Bake 25-30 minutes. Serve warm or cold with whipped cream.

Old-Fashioned Gingerbread
Joe Inman, Jr.

A 1970 graduate of Wake Forest University, Joe is one of the more enthusiastic people in the game of golf. He always has a good word for everyone; he has a secure attitude and is happy with his progress. This gingerbread should bring back lots of wonderful memories.

Yield: 1 9 × 9-inch cake

2 ¹/₃ cups unsifted whole wheat flour
1 ¹/₂ teaspoons baking powder
¹/₂ teaspoon salt
¹/₂ teaspoon baking soda
2 teaspoons ground ginger
1 ¹/₂ teaspoons cinnamon
¹/₂ teaspoon nutmeg
¹/₂ teaspoon allspice
¹/₂ cup soft butter
¹/₂ to ³/₄ cup light honey
2 tablespoons brown sugar
2 eggs
¹/₂ cup unsulphured molasses
1 cup hot water
1 cup raisins (optional)

Preheat oven to 350 degrees.
1. Sift together flour, baking powder and salt.
2. Blend together baking soda, spices and butter. Stir in the honey and brown sugar. Beat in the eggs. Stir in the molasses.
3. Add hot water alternately with the flour mixture to egg mixture. Add raisins.
4. Pour into well-buttered 9 × 9-inch pan and bake 45 minutes at 350 degrees.

 Excellent for breakfast.

Bob Hope's Favorite Lemon Pie   Bob Hope

Need we say more?

Yield: 1 9-inch pie

1 cup plus 2 tablespoons sugar
3 tablespoons cornstarch
1 cup boiling water
4 egg yolks
2 tablespoons butter
grated rind of 1 lemon
4 tablespoons lemon juice
pinch of salt
baked 9-inch pie crust
3 egg whites
2 tablespoons sugar

Preheat oven to 300 degrees.
1. Combine sugar and cornstarch. Add water slowly, stirring constantly, until thick and smooth.
2. Add slightly beaten egg yolks, butter, lemon rind and juice, and salt. Cook 2-3 minutes. Pour into baked shell.
3. Cover with meringue made from 3 egg whites, beaten stiff, and 2 tablespoons sugar.
4. Bake in a slow oven, at 300 degrees for 15 minutes or until light brown.

Pavlova   Jane Lock

Jane's amateur career was an international success story.
She won or was runner up in Australian, British, Canadian
and French events. As a native of Australia, Jane would like
you to try Pavlova, the national dessert of Australia.

Yield: 4 servings

4 egg whites (large eggs)
1 cup white sugar
1 teaspoon vinegar
½ teaspoon vanilla extract
1 teaspoon cornstarch

Preheat oven to 200 degrees.
1. Beat egg whites until stiff.
2. Add sugar gradually, beating all the time.
3. Add the vinegar and vanilla.
4. Add the cornstarch, at the end, gradually.
5. Turn on to a damp paper bag on a cookie sheet. Put on
   second rack from the bottom of oven.
6. Bake for 2-3 hours at 200 degrees. Must be crisp on top
   and marshmallowy inside.

Suggested Toppings: Whipped cream, decorated with
   strawberries. Chocolate cream, topped with grated
   chocolate.

Peanut Butter Pie   Lenore Muraoka

One of the LPGA's nine First-Try Champions in 1983,
Lenore won the Henredon Classic. She lives in Hawaii and
brings you her favorite pie.

3 ounces cream cheese, beaten fluffy
1 cup powdered sugar
⅓ cup peanut butter
½ cup milk
1 8-ounce container Cool Whip topping
1 prepared 8-inch graham cracker pie crust

1. Beat the cream cheese until fluffy and add the sugar, peanut butter and milk.
2. Gently fold in the Cool Whip topping.
3. Pour into graham cracker crust and put in freezer.
4. Top it off with more Cool Whip topping if desired.

Pecan Pie   Hale Irwin

Hale now lives in Frontenac, Missouri, with his wife, Sally, and their children. You never have to worry about this winner—a rich treat that makes an excellent finale for almost any menu.

Yield: 1 9-inch pie

3 eggs
½ cup sugar
dash of salt
1 teaspoon vanilla extract
1 cup dark Karo syrup
3 tablespoons melted butter, cooled
1 ⅓ cups pecans, whole
1 unbaked 9-inch pie crust

Preheat oven to 350 degrees.
1. Beat eggs with wire whisk.
2. Add rest of ingredients and mix well.
3. Pour into pie shell.
4. Bake at 350 degrees for 30 minutes or until pie is set.
   Serve with sweetened whipped cream.

Pineapple Lemon Pie
Leonard Thompson

Leonard Thompson understands calories since he lost nearly 50 pounds in 3½ months! Now his weight has stabilized and he enjoys eating good nutritious food. When he does splurge, it is with this lemon pie!

Yield: 1 9-inch pie

1 15-ounce can Eagle Brand Condensed Milk
⅓ cup lemon juice
1 6-ounce can crushed pineapple
½ pint whipping cream, whipped, or Cool Whip topping
1 prepared 9-inch graham cracker pie crust

1. Blend together the first 3 ingredients.
2. Pour into the graham cracker crust and top with cream.
3. Refrigerate until set.

♀ For ease in cutting a pie, first dip the knife in cold water.

Pots de Crème

Very impressive for something so easy.

Yield: 4 servings

¾ cup milk
1 6-ounce package chocolate chips
1 egg
2 tablespoons brandy, rum or crème de menthe
1 teaspoon sugar
whipped cream

1. Heat milk to a boil.
2. Put milk in blender with chocolate chips, egg, brandy, and sugar.
3. Blend 2 minutes; pour into small cups.
4. Serve chilled with whipped cream.

♀ Can be made just before dinner or earlier in the day.

Praline Pie   Phil Hancock

Phil and his wife, Kitty, invite you to indulge in this pie. A typical Florida recipe, this easy-to-assemble dessert will be your favorite, too. Phil has been working hard and his work will surely pay off in future tournaments.

Yield: 1 9-inch pie

⅓ cup butter
⅓ cup firmly packed brown sugar
½ cup chopped pecans
1 baked 9-inch pie shell
1 5-ounce package vanilla pudding-and-pie filling
2½ cups milk
1 envelope Dream Whip topping

Preheat oven to 400 degrees.
1. Combine butter, brown sugar and nuts in a saucepan; heat until butter and sugar are melted.
2. Spread on bottom of prepared pie shell. Bake at 400 degrees for 5 minutes or until bubbly; cool.
3. Prepare pie filling with milk as directed on package for pie. Remove 1 cup, cover, and chill thoroughly. Pour remaining filling into pie shell.
4. Prepare whipped topping mix as directed on package; blend 1⅓ cups into the 1 cup of reserved pie filling.
5. Spoon into pie shell; chill about 3 hours. Garnish with remaining whipped topping and pecans, if desired.

Pumpkin Cheesecake
Mike McCullough

Mike and Marilyn McCullough live in Scottsdale, Arizona, and love to entertain in small groups. Family is uppermost around holiday time and Mike's favorite Thanksgiving Day dessert is this cheesecake. It has a light, smooth, creamy texture.

Yield: 1 9-inch cake

1 8-ounce package cream cheese, softened
1 cup light cream
1 cup canned pumpkin*
3/4 cup sugar
4 eggs, separated
3 tablespoons all-purpose flour
1 teaspoon vanilla extract
1 teaspoon ground cinnamon
1/2 teaspoon ground ginger
1/2 teaspoon nutmeg
1/4 teaspoon salt
1 prepared 9-inch graham cracker pie crust

Preheat oven to 325 degrees.
1. In large mixer bowl, combine softened cream cheese with cream, pumpkin, sugar, egg yolks, flour, vanilla, cinnamon, ginger, nutmeg and salt. Beat until smooth.
2. Fold in stiffly beaten egg whites. Turn into prepared crust.
3. Bake at 325 degrees for 1 hour.

Optional Topping

1 cup sour cream
2 tablespoons sugar
1/2 teaspoon vanilla extract

1. Combine the sour cream, sugar and vanilla. Spread over cheesecake.
2. Bake 5 minutes more.

*Fresh cooked pumpkin may be substituted for canned.

Pumpkin Chiffon Pie Bob Gilder

The 1983 Phoenix Open winner, Bob plays out of the Carmel Valley Ranch, Carmel, California. Some people simply don't like pumpkin pie, but watch their expressions change when you serve this one!

Yield: 1 9-inch pie

Graham Cracker Coconut Crust

³/₄ cup graham cracker crumbs
³/₄ cup sweetened coconut
¹/₃ cup melted butter
¹/₄ cup finely chopped pecans
2 tablespoons sugar

Preheat oven to 375 degrees.
1. Mix all ingredients in medium bowl.
2. Press mixture evenly on bottom and sides of a 9-inch pie pan. Bake about 8 minutes.
3. Cool on rack.

Pie Filling

¹/₂ cup sugar
1 envelope unflavored gelatin
¹/₂ teaspoon salt
¹/₂ teaspoon ground cinnamon
¹/₄ teaspoon nutmeg
¹/₄ teaspoon ground ginger
3 eggs, separated
³/₄ cup milk
1 cup canned pumpkin
¹/₂ cup whipping cream, whipped

1. Mix sugar, gelatin, salt, cinnamon, nutmeg and ginger in top of 2-quart double boiler; stir in egg yolks and milk gradually.
2. Heat over, but not in, boiling water, stirring constantly until mixture thickens, about 20 minutes.
3. Remove from heat, stir in pumpkin. Refrigerate, covered, until partially set, about 30 minutes.

4. Beat egg whites in small bowl until stiff.
5. Whisk refrigerated gelatin mixture in large bowl to remove lumps. Fold ½ cup of the beaten egg whites into gelatin mixture, then fold in remaining egg whites. Pour into prepared crust.
6. Refrigerate until firm, at least 4 hours but not longer than 24 hours.
7. Spread whipped cream over pie.

Ritzy Cracker Pie   Frank Conner

Frank Conner is not only a golf professional, he's also a tennis pro. He didn't swing a club until he was 24 years old, having played tennis since he was ten. He decided to switch and has been winning ever since. Frank and his family now live in San Antonio, Texas.

Yield: 1 9-inch pie

3 egg whites
1 cup sugar
½ teaspoon baking powder
1 teaspoon vanilla extract
12 crushed Ritz crackers
1 cup chopped nuts (preferably pecans)
whipped cream for topping

Preheat oven to 375 degrees.
1. Beat egg whites until they peak.
2. Add sugar, baking powder, vanilla.
3. Fold in crackers and nuts.
4. Pour into a well-greased 9-inch pie pan.
5. Bake 30 minutes or longer at 375 degrees.
6. Cool and serve with whipped cream for topping.

Fresh Strawberry Soufflé

A fantasy come true.   (See photograph)

Yield: 8 servings

2 pints fresh strawberries, washed and hulled
2 envelopes unflavored gelatin
½ cup water
⅔ cup sugar
1 tablespoon lemon juice
4 egg whites (large eggs)
½ cup sugar (in addition to above sugar)
1 cup heavy cream

1. Mash strawberries in blender until puréed. Pour into large mixing bowl.
2. Combine gelatin, water, and first sugar in small saucepan. Cook over medium heat, stirring constantly, until gelatin is dissolved. Remove from heat and cool slightly.
3. Add lemon juice and gelatin mixture to strawberry purée. Chill until it is the consistency of unbeaten egg whites and mounds slightly when dropped from a spoon.
4. Beat egg whites until foamy; add second ½ cup sugar slowly while beating. Beat until stiff glossy peaks form. Fold into strawberry mixture.
5. Whip cream; fold into mixture. Pour into serving dish. Chill at least 4 hours until set or overnight.

Homemade Vanilla Ice Cream
Rick Pearson

Rick turned pro in 1980 after achieving the Florida State Amateur Championship. His special interests, aside from golf, include magic, computer programing, and music. Try making this ice cream and top it with some of Jim Simons' Hot Fudge Sauce, page 197.

Yield: About 1 quart

2 eggs
½ pint whipping cream
½ cup sugar
¼ teaspoon salt
1 tablespoon vanilla extract
1 15-ounce can Eagle Brand Condensed Milk
almost ½ quart milk

1. Combine eggs, whipping cream, sugar, salt and vanilla in large bowl and mix thoroughly with mixer.
2. Add condensed milk and stir well. Pour into freezing can.
3. Add milk and stir. Freeze according to directions, and enjoy.

 Mix ice and rock salt together to pack around can when freezing.

Whiskey Cake   Loren Roberts

Loren Roberts was born, educated and works in San Luis Obispo, California. He recently joined the PGA tour. Kim, Loren's wife, says this cake is perfect to serve with coffee or tea.

Yield: 1 bundt cake

1 package Duncan Hines Batter Mix
1/2 cup butter
1 5-ounce package vanilla instant pudding
4 eggs
1/2 cup half & half
1/2 cup ginger ale
1/4 cup toasted coconut
1 cup chopped nuts

Preheat oven to 350 degrees.
1. Mix together all ingredients.
2. Bake in greased bundt pan 50-60 minutes.

Topping

1/2 cup butter
1/4 cup sugar
1/4 cup apricot-flavored whiskey

After removing cake from oven, melt the butter, combine with the sugar and whiskey. Spread over the cake.

Chocolate Cookie Sheet Cake

Hal Sutton

Hal is the winner of the 1983 PGA Championship. He turned professional in 1981 and in his first two years on the tour, he has won more events than any player since Jack Nicklaus blossomed onto the scene.

Yield: 13 × 9-inch cake

2 cups flour
2 cups sugar
1/2 teaspoon salt
1 cup water
1 stick butter
1 cup shortening
3 tablespoons cocoa
2 eggs
1/2 cup buttermilk
1/2 teaspoon baking soda
1 teaspoon vanilla extract

Preheat oven to 350 degrees.
1. In a bowl, mix together the flour, sugar and salt.
2. In a saucepan, mix together the water, butter, shortening and cocoa; bring to a boil, stirring constantly.
3. Pour over flour mixture and stir well.
4. Add the eggs, buttermilk, soda, and vanilla extract. Beat well.
5. Pour into a 13 × 9-inch pan and bake for 20 minutes at 350 degrees.

Icing

1 stick butter
6 tablespoons milk (sweet)
3 tablespoons cocoa
1 box powdered sugar
1 teaspoon vanilla extract
1/2 cup nuts

Bring butter and milk to a boil. Add cocoa, sugar, vanilla and nuts and ice cake while still warm.

Chocolate Soufflé Viennese
Low Fat

Richly deserved with low-fat elegance.

Yield: 6 servings (85 calories each)

1 ½ tablespoons butter or margarine, melted
4 teaspoons liquid sweetener
1 ½ tablespoons flour
½ cup skim milk
3 tablespoons cocoa
3 eggs, separated
1 ½ teaspoons vanilla extract
¼ teaspoon cream of tartar

Preheat oven to 350 degrees.
1. Combine butter and liquid sweetener; set over low heat until butter is melted; blend in flour.
2. Add milk; stir over medium heat until it thickens. Add cocoa.
3. Beat egg yolks; add vanilla. Add hot sauce slowly. Add cream of tartar to egg whites; beat until stiff.
4. Fold into egg-yolk mixture. Pour into ungreased 1-quart baking dish. Set in pan of warm water and bake in a 350-degree oven about 45 minutes or until firm.

Watermelon Mousse   Low Fat

A low-fat dessert that tastes really special.

Yield: 8 servings (24 calories each)

1 quart watermelon pulp and juice
2 tablespoons cornstarch
6 sweetener tablets, mashed
¼ teaspoon cinnamon
½ teaspoon vanilla extract
1 tablespoon chopped citron
2 tablespoons grated coconut

1. Cut watermelon from rind. Cube. Mash to a thin pulp. Rub through a sieve, discarding seeds. Extract enough pulp and juice to make 1 quart.
2. Place pulp and juice in saucepan.
3. Blend together cornstarch, sweetener and cinnamon. Slowly stir into watermelon juice.
4. Cook over low heat about 10 minutes, stirring constantly. When ready, mixture should coat the spoon. Remove and add vanilla and citron. Beat until smooth.
5. Pour into sherbet glasses, top with coconut. Place in refrigerator until solid.

OOOOOOOOOOOOOOOOOOOOOO

Cookies and Candies

OOOOOOOOOOOOOOOOOOOOOO

After Golf Cookies   Kathryn Crosby

A family favorite.

Yield: About 36 cookies

2 ½ cups unsifted flour
1 teaspoon baking soda
1 teaspoon salt
1 cup butter or margarine
1 cup white sugar
1 cup brown sugar
1 teaspoon vanilla extract
2 eggs
1 12-ounce package chocolate or butterscotch chips
1 cup broken, roasted, salted nut meats
1 cup coconut

Preheat oven to 375 degrees.
1. On waxed paper, combine flour, baking soda and salt.
2. In mixing bowl, combine butter, sugar and vanilla. Beat until creamy. Beat in eggs.
3. Gradually add flour mixture and mix well. Stir in chocolate or butterscotch chips, nut meats and coconut.
4. Drop by teaspoon onto lightly greased cookie sheet.
5. Bake at 375 degrees for 16-20 minutes.

 Can be frozen.

Cheesecake Bars   Ben D. Crenshaw

A big hit among big hitters! "Gentle Ben" loves bird watching to get away from the game for a while. A Million Dollar Winner in career earnings since 1973, Ben has always been a gallery pleaser. His tour victories include the 1983 Byron Nelson Classic.

Yield: 16 bars

1 cup flour
1/3 cup packed brown sugar
6 tablespoons margarine, softened
1 8-ounce package cream cheese, softened
1/4 cup sugar
2 tablespoons milk
1 egg
1/4 teaspoon finely shredded lemon peel
2 tablespoons lemon juice
1/2 teaspoon vanilla extract
2 tablespoons chopped walnuts

Preheat oven to 350 degrees.
1. Combine flour and sugar. Cut in margarine until it forms fine crumbs.
2. Reserve 1 cup of crumbs for topping. Press remainder over bottom of ungreased 8 × 8 × 2-inch pan.
3. Bake at 350 degrees for 12-15 minutes, until light brown.
4. Thoroughly cream together cream cheese and sugar. Add milk, egg, lemon peel, lemon juice and vanilla. Beat well.
5. Spread over slightly cooled crust. Combine walnuts with remaining crumb mixture and sprinkle over pan.
6. Bake at 350 degrees for 20-25 minutes. Cool before cutting.

This recipe can easily be doubled.

Put a piece of apple in your brown sugar jar to keep it from drying out and lumping.

Chocolate Oatmeal Bars

John Fought, Jr.

A product of Brigham Young University, John has teetered between golf and accounting. He finally decided in favor of golf and is now on the road to golf stardom. John and his wife, Donna, recommend these cookies for breakfast, lunch and/or dinner—very rich and very good!

Yield: 24 squares

12 ounces semi-sweet chocolate chips
²/₃ cup condensed milk
4 teaspoons vanilla extract
1 cup margarine
1 cup light brown sugar
²/₃ cup white sugar
2 eggs
1 ¹/₃ cups flour
4 cups quick oatmeal
1 cup chopped nuts

Preheat oven to 350 degrees.
1. Melt chocolate chips with milk and 2 teaspoons vanilla in the top of a double boiler.
2. Cream margarine with sugar. Add eggs and remaining 2 teaspoons vanilla and mix together.
3. Stir in flour and oatmeal. Place ²/₃ of mixture on bottom layer of a greased 9 × 13 × 2-inch Pyrex dish.
4. Add chopped nuts to remaining ¹/₃ of oatmeal mixture and beat together.
5. Pour chocolate mixture over layer of oatmeal mixture in Pyrex dish.
6. Crumble remaining mixture over chocolate.
7. Bake at 350 degrees for 30 minutes. When cool, cut into small squares.

Great Pumpkin Cookies
Bobby Nichols

Charlie Brown's favorite, too!! Bobby limits his traveling now and will soon join the senior tour. It has been a wonderful career, especially for a man who was almost unable to play at all due to injuries. His special interests now are sport and antique cars.

Yield: 32 large cookies

4 cups unsifted all-purpose flour
2 cups quick or old-fashioned rolled oats (uncooked)
2 teaspoons baking soda
2 teaspoons ground cinnamon
1 teaspoon salt
1½ cups butter or margarine (softened)
2 cups firmly packed brown sugar
1 cup granulated sugar
1 egg
1 teaspoon vanilla extract
1 16-ounce can solid-pack pumpkin
1 cup semi-sweet chocolate morsels
assorted icings or peanut butter
assorted candies, raisins, or nuts

Preheat oven to 350 degrees.
1. Combine flour, oats, soda, cinnamon and salt; set aside.
2. Cream butter; gradually add sugars, beating until light and fluffy. Add egg and vanilla; mix well.
3. Add dry ingredients and pumpkin alternately, mixing well after each addition. Stir in morsels.
4. For each cookie, drop ¼-cup dough onto lightly greased cookie sheet; spread into pumpkin shape using a thin metal spatula. Add a bit more dough to form stem.
5. Bake at 350 degrees 20-25 minutes until cookies are firm and lightly browned.
6. Remove from cookie sheets; cool on racks.
7. Decorate, using icing or peanut butter to affix assorted candies, raisins, or nuts.

Ice Box Cookies

Helen Goalby (Bob's Mother)

Nothing is better than cookies that Mother used to make!
Bob, now on the senior tour, does on-course analyzing for
NBC golf telecasts.

Yield: 36 cookies

2 cups sugar (1 cup white, 1 cup brown)
1/2 cup butter
2 eggs, beaten
3 cups flour
1 teaspoon cream of tartar
1/4 teaspoon salt
1 teaspoon baking soda in 1 tablespoon hot water
1 teaspoon vanilla extract
chopped pecans (optional)

Preheat oven to 350 degrees.
1. Mix all ingredients in large bowl.
2. Mold dough into small 2-inch rolls and chill overnight.
3. Slice rolls 1/4-inch thick; place on greased cookie sheet
   and bake in a 350-degree oven until golden brown,
   about 10-12 minutes.

Mandel Bread

A not-too-sweet dry cookie with an almond flavor.

Yield: About 36 cookies

¹/₂ cup butter
2 tablespoons shortening (Crisco)
1 cup sugar
3 eggs
3 cups flour
¹/₂ teaspoon baking soda
1 teaspoon baking powder
1 cup chopped walnuts
1 teaspoon vanilla extract
1 teaspoon almond extract
sugar and cinnamon

Preheat oven to 350 degrees.
1. Cream the butter, Crisco and sugar.
2. Add the eggs, one at a time, and beat well; it must be smooth.
3. Add the flour, soda and baking powder, which have been sifted together beforehand. Batter will be thick.
4. Add walnuts and vanilla and almond extract.
5. Divide in half and shape into long rolls on an ungreased cookie sheet. Sprinkle with cinnamon and sugar prior to baking.
6. Bake at 350 degrees for 20 to 25 minutes.
7. While still hot, slice into 1-inch slices, at an angle, and brown under the broiler.

Monster Cookies

Boo!!!

Yield: 36 monsters

3 eggs
½ cup margarine
1 cup brown sugar
1 cup white sugar
1 teaspoon vanilla extract
1 ¼ cups crunchy peanut butter
2 teaspoons baking soda
4 ½ cups minute oatmeal
1 cup chocolate chips

Preheat oven to 350 degrees.
1. Mix all ingredients together in large bowl until well blended.
2. On greased cookie sheet, spoon out ¼ cup cookie dough per cookie. Flatten. Bake for 10 minutes.
3. Let cool on cookie sheet at least 5 minutes before serving.
4. After cookies have cooled, wrap each one in plastic wrap. Place on a cold oven rack. Put in oven for 30 seconds at 300 degrees. This seals the wrapping so that the cookies stay moist and fresh.

Spidery Haystack Cookies
Mark Coward

My, how they seem to "crawl" out of the cookie jar. A perfect reward for children and adults.

Yield: 36 cookies

6 ounces chocolate chips
1 12-ounce package butterscotch morsels
2 tablespoons peanut butter
1 5-ounce can Chinese noodles
1 12-ounce package salted peanuts

1. Melt chocolate, butterscotch and peanut butter in micro-wave or over water in a double boiler.
2. Stir in noodles and peanuts.
3. Drop by teaspoons on waxed paper. Let set until firm.
4. Store in airtight container.

My Favorite Chocolate Bar
Amy Alcott

This chocolate treat is as good as dropping that pressure putt for the "big win." Amy lives in Pacific Palisades, California, and loves to spend her free time in the kitchen.

Yield: 16-20 bars

½ cup butter
1 cup graham cracker crumbs
1 cup coconut
1 cup chocolate chips
1 cup chopped nuts
1 cup Eagle Brand Milk

Preheat oven to 350 degrees.
1. Melt the butter in a 9 × 9-inch baking pan.
2. Sprinkle the graham cracker crumbs over the butter.
3. Sprinkle the coconut over the graham cracker crumbs.
4. Sprinkle the chocolate chips over the coconut.
5. Over this, sprinkle the chopped nuts.
6. Now, over this entire concoction, dribble the Eagle Brand Milk.
7. Bake at 350 degrees for 30 minutes. Cool and cut into bars. Yumm! The Best!!

Chocolate Peanut Butter Balls

"No topping" this one.

Yield: About 36 balls

1 cup chopped dates
1 cup chopped walnuts
1 cup powdered sugar, sifted
1 cup chunky peanut butter
2 tablespoons butter, melted
12 squares semi-sweet chocolate

1. Line baking sheets with waxed paper.
2. Combine dates and walnuts in large bowl. Add powdered sugar. Blend in peanut butter and melted butter and mix thoroughly. Shape into 1 to 1½-inch balls.
3. Melt chocolate in top of double boiler set over hot water, stirring occasionally to prevent lumping.
4. Dip balls into chocolate with fork, turning to coat evenly. Transfer to baking sheets.
5. Refrigerate until chocolate is set, about 1 hour. Candies can be placed in miniature muffin cup liners. Refrigerate candies until ready to serve.

Frozen Chocolate Frangos

Almost sinful!

Yield: 12 servings

1 cup butter
2 cups sifted powdered sugar
4 squares unsweetened chocolate, melted
4 eggs
¾ teaspoon peppermint flavoring
2 teaspoons vanilla extract
1 cup crushed vanilla wafers

1. Beat butter and sugar in electric mixer until fluffy.
2. Add melted chocolate, eggs, and flavorings; beat well.
3. Insert paper liners into muffin tin. Put some vanilla wafer crumbs in each; fill with chocolate mixture.
4. Sprinkle a few more crumbs on top and freeze.
5. Remove from freezer about 10 to 15 minutes before serving.

Carmel-by-the-Sea's Fudge

The "too-good-to-be-true" variety.

Yield: 1 9 × 13-inch panful

4½ cups granulated sugar
1 13-ounce can evaporated milk
1 cup butter
3 cups milk chocolate chips*
1 7-ounce jar marshmallow creme
2 squares bittersweet chocolate
3 tablespoons vinegar
1 cup chopped nuts (optional)

1. Mix together the sugar, milk and butter; heat slowly to soft-ball stage (238 degrees) using a candy thermometer. Stir constantly so that it does not stick.
2. When it reaches the soft-ball stage, remove from heat and add milk chocolate chips, marshmallow creme, bittersweet chocolate and vinegar.
3. Stir until creamy.
4. Add chopped nuts if desired. Pour into a greased 9 × 13 × 2-inch pan.

*Very important to use milk chocolate chips.

Fudge Nut Drops

You'd have to be nuts *not* to love these!!

Yield: About 72 pieces

²/₃ cup cocoa, unsweetened
1 ¹/₃ cups sugar
1 cup milk
2 12-ounce packages peanut butter chips
2 teaspoons vanilla extract
2 teaspoons rum flavoring
1 cup chopped walnuts, pecans, or cashews

1. In a saucepan combine cocoa, sugar, milk and chips. Stir constantly over low heat until chips are melted and mixture is smooth.
2. Stir in vanilla and rum flavoring. Fold in nuts. Cool until mixture holds its shape.
3. Drop mixture in lumps about the size of a large olive onto foil-lined cookie sheets. Chill until hard.
4. Store in airtight containers in a cool dry place.

Larry's Mom's Oatmeal Fudge   Larry Nelson

Thanks, Mom! An interesting recipe you eat out of the bowl or with your fingers. Larry loves a challenge—the bigger the better. Larry and his family live in Marietta, Georgia, and he is affiliated with La Quinta Hotel and Golf Club, La Quinta, California.

Yield: 50-60 pieces

2 cups sugar
4 tablespoons cocoa
¹/₂ cup evaporated milk
¹/₄ cup white Karo syrup
1 stick butter
2 cups oatmeal
¹/₂ cup peanut butter
1 teaspoon vanilla extract

1. Mix sugar, cocoa, milk, Karo syrup and butter.
2. Bring to rolling boil, stirring constantly. Cook 1 minute more after beginning to boil.
3. Remove from heat; immediately stir in oatmeal, peanut butter and vanilla. Stir as mixture cools; it thickens rapidly.
4. Eat it by the spoonful or cut into squares.

Grasshopper Balls

Yield: About 48 balls

¹/₂ cup light corn syrup
¹/₄ cup crème de menthe
3 tablespoons crème de cacao
2 8¹/₂-ounce packages chocolate wafers, crushed to 4¹/₄ cups
¹/₂ cup ground almonds
slivered almonds

1. In medium bowl, stir together corn syrup, crème de menthe, and crème de cacao. Add wafer crumbs, stirring until ingredients are moistened.
2. With hands, knead mixture until well mixed. Form into 1-inch balls; roll in ground almonds. Press one slivered almond into top of each.
3. Store in tightly covered container at least 1 week to blend flavors.

Marshmallow Log Candies

Easy and very colorful.

Yield: 24-36 slices

3 squares chocolate, melted
1 cup powdered sugar
½ cup chopped nuts
1 teaspoon lemon juice
1 teaspoon vanilla extract
1 package miniature colored marshmallows
1 7-ounce package flaked coconut

1. Mix all ingredients well, except the coconut.
2. Sprinkle coconut on waxed paper and roll mixture on coconut, into 2 log-shaped strips.
3. Freeze. When ready to use, cut in slices.

 When you have to cut marshmallows, use a pair of scissors dipped in hot water.

Minted Nuts

You will love these!

Yield: Over 1 pound

1 cup sugar
¹/₂ cup water
¹/₄ cup light corn syrup
10 large marshmallows
1 teaspoon peppermint extract
10 drops green food coloring
3 cups walnut or pecan halves

1. In heavy 2-quart saucepan, mix sugar, water and corn syrup.
2. Stirring constantly, bring to boil over medium heat. Continue cooking, stirring occasionally until temperature on candy thermometer reaches soft-ball stage (238 degrees). Remove from heat.
3. Stir in marshmallows and peppermint extract. Stir until marshmallows are melted. Add nuts and stir until well coated. Turn onto waxed paper.
4. With two forks, separate nuts while still warm. Cool several hours or until set.
5. Store in tightly covered containers.

Kahlua-Dipped Strawberries

Yield: About 20 pieces

1 square semi-sweet chocolate
¹/₂ cup sugar
¹/₂ cup hot coffee
2 tablespoons cornstarch dissolved in 1 tablespoon
**   cold water and 1 tablespoon Kahlua liqueur**
3 tablespoons Kahlua liqueur
2-3 baskets fresh strawberries

1. Mix chocolate, sugar and coffee in heavy saucepan.
2. Stir constantly over medium heat until chocolate melts and sugar dissolves.
3. Add cornstarch mixture; stir until very thick.
4. Remove from heat, add remaining Kahlua. Mix well. Cool. Makes about 1 cup.
5. Make sure berries are dry and hand dip individually.

Fancy Lace Cookies Low Fat

Elaborately embroidered.

Yield: 24 cookies (27 calories each)

1 egg
¼ cup sugar
3 teaspoons liquid sweetener
¼ teaspoon vanilla extract
¼ teaspoon almond extract
1 teaspoon unsalted butter
½ cup rolled oats
¼ cup chopped, roasted chestnuts
¼ cup shredded coconut

Preheat oven to 375 degrees.
1. Beat egg until light.
2. Add sugar, sweetener, vanilla, and almond extract, and beat together.
3. Add butter, oats, nuts and coconut. Blend all ingredients.
4. Drop on lightly buttered cookie sheet.
5. Flatten individual cookies with a knife.
6. Bake in a 375-degree oven until well browned.

Charlotte Russe   Low Fat

Low-calorie excellence.

Yield: 10 servings (58 calories each)

Ladyfingers

3 eggs, separated
1 ½ tablespoons sugar
2 teaspoons liquid sweetener
1 teaspoon vanilla extract
½ cup flour, sifted

Preheat oven to 350 degrees.
1. Beat egg whites until stiff. Add sugar and sweetener.
2. Beat egg yolks until thickened and lemon colored; add the vanilla, fold into egg whites.
3. Fold in flour a small amount at a time.
4. Shape on ungreased cookie sheet that has been covered with lightly greased foil. Using 2 tablespoons for each ladyfinger, make each about 1 inch wide and 3 inches long. Smooth tops with spatula.
5. Bake in a 350-degree oven for 12 minutes. Cool. Remove with spatula. Makes about 20 ladyfingers.

Filling

2 envelopes gelatin, unflavored
1 cup cold water
6 tablespoons cocoa
4 teaspoons liquid sweetener
3 cups hot water

1. Sprinkle gelatin on cold water. Add cocoa and sweetener to gelatin; mix well.
2. Add hot water slowly, blending thoroughly.
3. Chill until consistency of unbeaten egg white. Then whip until frothy. Chill until mixture will heap slightly on spoon.
4. Line 8 or 9-inch pan with ladyfingers. Ladle chocolate mixture into center. Chill until firm.

○○○○○○○○○○○○○○○○○○○○○

The 19th Hole Beverages

○○○○○○○○○○○○○○○○○○○○○

Drunken Apricots

Drown your sorrows and tomorrows.

Yield: 1 serving

apricots
1 ½ ounces Southern Comfort
champagne
ice cubes

1. Freeze apricots into ice cubes with water, chopping apricots into smaller pieces, if necessary.
2. Put ice cubes with frozen apricots into wine glass.
3. Add Southern Comfort, filling the rest of the glass with champagne.

Banana Daiquiri

A guaranteed success!

Yield: 6 servings

2 cups ice cubes or crushed ice or shaved ice
¾ cup light rum
½ cup sweet & sour mix
½ cup half & half
¼ cup Triple Sec or Curacao
2 very ripe medium bananas
orange slices for garnish

1. Put ice into blender.
2. Add remaining ingredients except orange slices and blend on high for about 1½ minutes. Serve in stemmed glasses; garnish with the orange slices.

Champagne Punch

Smart sparkle...an effervescent energizer!

Yield: About 30 servings

1 6-ounce package lime-flavored gelatin
6 cups boiling water
2 cups sugar
2 46-ounce cans unsweetened pineapple juice
2 quarts ginger ale
1-1½ bottles champagne

1. Dissolve gelatin in boiling water.
2. Add sugar and pineapple juice.
3. Freeze in mold until firm.
4. Remove from freezer about 3 hours before using. Place in punch bowl and add the ginger ale and champagne to serve.

Christmas Punch

Yield: About 25 cups

1 46-ounce can unsweetened pineapple juice
1 46-ounce can unsweetened grapefruit juice
½ gallon cranberry juice
1 12-ounce can frozen orange juice, undiluted
1 28-ounce bottle lemon-lime soda
2 cups bourbon

1. Eight hours before serving, mix all ingredients.
2. Just before serving, add ice.

Coffee Royale Punch

Yield: 30 servings

2 quarts coffee
½ cup rum (the more the merrier)
2 quarts vanilla ice cream

1. Freeze coffee into ice cube trays.
2. Just before serving, run the cubes through an ice crusher.
3. Put all ingredients into a punch bowl; stir until most of the ice is melted and all is blended into a smooth, rich punch.

♀ To serve 40 people, use 1 pound of coffee and 10 quarts of water.

Dutch Treat

This after-dinner coffee is lovely for guests or as a treat for yourself!

Yield: 1 serving

½ cup plus 2 tablespoons hot black coffee
1 teaspoon sugar
2 tablespoons brandy
2 tablespoons chocolate-mint liqueur
1 twist of lemon

1. Pour coffee into preheated 8-ounce mug and stir in sugar.
2. Add brandy and liqueur and stir again. Twist lemon over the top and drop in.

♀ Don't throw out left-over coffee! Freeze it into coffee ice cubes for use in iced coffee. Same goes for iced tea.

Irish Coffee   Microwave

Serve in tall glass mugs.

Yield: 1 serving

1 teaspoon sugar
1 cup strong coffee
1 jigger Irish whiskey
1 spoonful whipped cream

1. Mix sugar and coffee in large cup or mug.
2. Microwave on High for 1½ to 2 minutes or until hot.
3. Add Irish whiskey. Top with whipped cream and serve.

"Special" Colada   Mark McCumber

Mark serves these at parties.

Yield: 4 servings

2 bananas, sliced
1 8-ounce package frozen strawberries
1 6-ounce can frozen lemon and limeade juice
rum to taste (be generous…makes for a lively
party!)

1. Place all ingredients in blender.
2. Add enough crushed ice to fill blender. Blend.

Eggnog

Your basic holiday elixir.

Yield: 2 quarts

12 egg yolks
pinch of salt
¾ cup sugar
1 cup bourbon or dark rum
12 egg whites, stiffly beaten
1 pint whipping cream, whipped

1. In a bowl, beat yolks, adding salt and sugar slowly.
2. Add bourbon or rum, very slowly, while beating.
3. Fold in whites, then fold in cream. Chill before serving.

19th Hole Frozen Margarita
Mark Coward

Sit back and lie about your game! (See photograph)

Yield: 2 servings

1 6-ounce can limeade, undiluted
½ cup Triple Sec
1 ½ cups tequila
ice

1. Mix ingredients in blender, add ice and liquefy.
2. Add ice until mixture is of desired consistency.
3. Salt glasses; pour in margaritas.

 These can be made ahead and kept in the refrigerator.

Hot Buttered Rum

This will warm up a cold round.

Yield: 4 quarts

¼ pound butter
1 pound dark brown sugar
¼ teaspoon ground cinnamon
¼ teaspoon ground cloves
¼ teaspoon nutmeg
1 bottle rum
3 quarts water

1. Cream butter with brown sugar.*
2. Mix in cinnamon, cloves and nutmeg.
3. Add the rum and water and heat.

*The butter-sugar mixture can be done ahead of time.

White Sangria

Good to the last bubble! (See photograph)

Yield: 4-6 servings

1 orange
1 fifth dry white wine
2 slices lemon
2 slices lime
1 ounce cognac
2 tablespoons sugar
1 stick cinnamon
8 large strawberries, hulled and halved
ice cubes

1. Cut entire peel of orange in a single strip. The white part should be cut along with outer peel so that orange fruit is exposed.
2. Carefully place orange in glass pitcher, fastening top end of peel over rim. Pour wine into pitcher. Add remaining ingredients. Stir gently to dissolve sugar.
3. Let mixture set at room temperature at least 1 hour.
4. Add 1 tray of ice cubes immediately before serving; stir.

The Separator

You will be able to tell the men from the boys!

Yield: 1 serving

1 1/2 ounces Kahlua
1 ounce half & half
1 ounce brandy

1. Into a 5-ounce highball glass, pour the Kahlua.
2. Slowly float the half & half on top.
3. On top of that, float the brandy. Be sure to float the last 2 ingredients carefully to create the separator effect.

Siberian Souse

Yield: 1 serving

1 whole fresh apricot, blanched and peeled or one
  whole canned apricot, well drained
2 tablespoons fresh lemon juice
2 tablespoons vodka
2 tablespoons apricot brandy
crushed ice
sparking mineral water or club soda

1. Pierce apricot on all sides with fork.
2. Place in bottom of large, chilled, wine glass.
3. Pour lemon juice, vodka and brandy over apricot and
   stir gently.
4. Fill glass with crushed ice and a splash of soda. Serve
   with small straw.

Silver Fizz

Best served at brunch.

Yield: 4 servings

²/₃ can frozen sweetened lemonade
6 ounces gin
6 ounces half & half
2 eggs
crushed ice
sparkling water

1. Mix lemonade, gin, half & half, and eggs together in
   blender.
2. Add ice and blend again. Serve in 4 tall glasses over ice
   cubes and top with sparkling water.

Zippy Tom

Good to the last shot!

Yield: 4 servings

1 quart tomato juice
4 lemons
1 teaspoon chili powder
pepper
garlic powder
French's Herb Seasoning
4 celery stalk tips, with leaves

1. Combine tomato juice, the juice of the lemons, and chili powder.
2. Season to taste with pepper, garlic powder and herb seasoning. Serve with stalk of celery in each glass.

Tom and Jerrys

A special holiday drink.

Yield: 12 servings

12 eggs, separated
1 ½ teaspoons ground cinnamon
½ teaspoon ground cloves
½ teaspoon allspice
4 cups granulated sugar
1 ½ ounces rum

1. Beat egg whites until stiff; add yolks.
2. Mix well and add spices and sugar. Add rum slowly, beating continually. It will become very thick.
3. Cover and store in refrigerator.

When ready to serve, to each cup add:

1 shot rum
¼ cup already prepared mixture
hot milk to fill cup

Sprinkle with nutmeg and enjoy.

Holiday Wassail

Serve this warm. Use oranges and cinnamon sticks as garnish in the punch bowl.

Yield: About 18 cups

3 large oranges
72 whole cloves
1 gallon apple juice
½ cup lemon juice
10 cinnamon sticks
2 cups vodka
¼ cup brandy

Preheat oven to 350 degrees.
1. Stud oranges with cloves. Bake uncovered in shallow pan at 350 degrees for 30 minutes.
2. Heat apple juice until bubbly at edge. Add lemon juice, cinnamon sticks and baked oranges. Simmer, uncovered, 30 minutes.
3. Remove from heat. Add vodka and brandy. Mix well.

OOOOOOOOOOOOOOOOOOOOO

Recipes from Noted Restaurants

OOOOOOOOOOOOOOOOOOOOO

Herbed Goat Cheese

The Cypress Room, The Lodge at Pebble Beach

Yield: 6 servings

1 11-ounce Montrachet log
¹/₂ cup chopped fresh herbs (parsley, dill, oregano, chives, thyme)
¹/₄ cup olive oil

1. Chill the cheese to firm it for slicing. Unwrap and cut with a sharp, wet knife into 6 slices.
2. Mix the chopped herbs in a bowl and roll each cheese slice in the mixture until it is completely covered.
3. Place the herbed cheese on a serving platter and drizzle the olive oil over the top.
4. Let the cheese warm to room temperature and serve with a crusty bread.

Cream of Asparagus Soup
Hog's Breath Inn, Carmel-by-the-Sea

Yield: 10-12 servings

15 asparagus spears, fresh
2 stalks celery
1 onion
1 pound butter
3 cups flour
½ quart chicken stock
½ quart whipping cream
½ quart milk
salt and pepper to taste
1 ounce Worcestershire sauce

1. Cut tips from asparagus; grind the asparagus, celery stalks, and onion. Sauté in a little butter until lightly cooked.
2. Add rest of butter; add flour and cook until light golden brown.
3. Add chicken stock and bring to a light simmer.
4. Add whipping cream and milk.
5. Sauté asparagus tips and mix into soup. Season to taste with salt, pepper and Worcestershire sauce.

San Francisco Cioppino

The Cypress Room, The Lodge at Pebble Beach

Yield: 4-6 servings

¼ cup olive oil
1 large onion, chopped
1 green pepper, seeded and chopped
2 cloves garlic, chopped
¼ pound mushrooms, sliced
1 bay leaf
4 cups fish stock
1 cup dry red wine
1 pound raw shrimp
2 rock lobster tails, cut into 1-inch slices
16 mussels, cleaned and scrubbed
16 littleneck clams, cleaned and scrubbed
2 pounds sea bass, cleaned and scaled and cut
    into 1-inch slices
salt
ground black pepper

1. In a large, heavy kettle or Dutch oven, heat the oil over
   medium heat. When it is hot, sauté the onion, green
   peppers and garlic until golden.
2. Add the mushrooms and sauté for 1 minute.
3. Add the bay leaf, stock and wine, and bring to a boil
   over high heat.
4. Lower the heat and add the shellfish and sea bass. Cover
   and simmer for 5 to 10 minutes or until the seafood is
   cooked.
5. Season to taste with salt and pepper; remove the bay
   leaf.

Gazpacho Soup
Whaling Station Inn, Monterey

Soup should have bits of vegetables in evidence. It is like a Bloody Mary and very tasty.

Yield: 4 servings

3 cups whole tomatoes, canned
½ cucumber, peeled and finely diced
½ small white onion, finely diced
1 stalk celery, finely diced
¼ lime, with rind
¼ (or less) orange, with rind
1 tablespoon Worcestershire sauce
salt and pepper to taste
pinch of cumin
pinch of chili powder
1 tablespoon cider vinegar
pinch of coriander
croutons

1. Drain off some of the juice from canned tomatoes. Crush tomatoes into thumbnail-sized pieces.
2. Add cucumber, onion, and celery.
3. Emulsify lime and orange pieces, with rinds, in blender or food processor. Add to tomatoes. Season with Worcestershire sauce, salt and pepper, cumin, chili powder, coriander and vinegar. Blend well and chill.
4. Serve very cold, with croutons.

Sparkling Cold Papaya Soup

The Covey at Quail Lodge, Carmel Valley

Yield: 10-12 servings

4 pounds papaya, crushed
3 cups orange juice
1 cup lime juice
1 cup guava honey
4 1/2 cups dry white wine
1 1/2 cups chilled sparkling water
kiwi fruit or strawberries for garnish

1. Combine papaya, juices and honey in blender until smooth.
2. Stir in wine and chill.
3. Place 6 ounces of soup into chilled serving dishes.
4. Garnish with kiwi fruit or strawberries and splash with 1 ounce of sparkling water.

Artichoke Vinaigrette
Whaling Station Inn, Monterey

Yield: 4 servings

4 medium artichokes
water to cook
1 clove garlic, crushed
1 bay leaf
salt and pepper to taste
½ lemon

1. Place trimmed artichokes, close together, in a pot of water measuring halfway to their tops. Add garlic, bay leaf, salt and pepper to water. Squeeze in lemon juice, then drop in whole lemon rind. Cover.
2. Cook over medium heat until done; test with a fork inserted into artichoke heart—it should be tender, but not mushy.
3. Drain and squeeze out extra water from artichokes. "Flowerette" by striking top of each artichoke with the palm of your hand; push downward to form an open flower. Cut out the "beard." Place on round dishes and dress with Vinaigrette Dressing.

Vinaigrette Dressing

¾ cup olive oil
¼ cup wine vinegar
¼ teaspoon dry mustard or Dijon mustard
a drop of catsup (optional)
few drops of Tabasco sauce to taste
1 anchovy fillet, mashed*
pepper to taste
pinch of sugar
1 clove garlic, mashed or diced very fine

Mix and chill well before using.

> *Anchovy replaces salt. But, taste before adding it all. You must satisfy your personal taste. Remember, saltiness may be added, but never taken away!

Nepenthe Bean Salad
Nepenthe, Big Sur

Yield: 4 servings

1 15-ounce can kidney beans
1 15-ounce can garbanzo beans
¾ cup oil
¾ cup red-wine vinegar
3 or 4 green onions, chopped
¼ teaspoon sugar
1 teaspoon salt
½ teaspoon black pepper
1 teaspoon tarragon
1 teaspoon oregano
1 teaspoon granulated garlic

1. Drain beans and rinse.
2. Mix all ingredients in large glass bowl.

♀ Tastes even better if marinated overnight.

Whaling Station Inn Salad

Whaling Station Inn, Monterey

Yield: 4 servings

½ head Romaine lettuce
1 small head Bibb lettuce
1 head Belgian endive
½ cup chopped walnut meats
1 bunch watercress

1. Wash and dry leaves of lettuce, endive and watercress. Crisp in refrigerator until ready to use.
2. Mix in walnut meats, and toss lightly with Special Olive Oil Dressing.

Special Olive Oil Dressing

¾ cup Marsala brand virgin cold-press olive oil*
⅛ cup rice vinegar**
⅛ cup cider vinegar
dash lemon juice
dash Worcestershire sauce
¼ teaspoon dry mustard

Blend well and use as directed.

*What is so special about this dressing is the olive oil. It is made by Sciabica & Sons, Modesto, California, a Sicilian family whose olive oil is sold in groceries and health food stores under the "Marsala" brand. This is the finest oil available.

**And, there is no better vinegar than rice vinegar to go with it.

Veal Cardinal

Sardine Factory, Monterey

Yield: 6 servings

6 6-ounce Australian lobster tails
1 ½ pounds veal (Wisconsin white veal from short
**   loin) cut in thin slices**
flour
2 tablespoons butter
1 ½ pounds fresh mushrooms, washed and sliced
½ cup sauterne wine
2 tablespoons fresh, chopped parsley
2 tablespoons fresh, chopped garlic
juice of one lemon
salt and pepper to taste

1. Dip the lobster and veal in flour. Heat the butter in a skillet and sauté the lobster lightly.
2. Add the mushrooms and continue cooking until the mushrooms are tender.
3. Remove the lobster and mushrooms with a slotted spoon and set aside.
4. Sauté the veal until golden brown on both sides, adding more butter if necessary. Return the lobster and mushrooms to the skillet.
5. Add the wine and touch with a lighted match.
6. When the flames have subsided, add the parsley, garlic, and lemon juice. Simmer for 2 to 3 minutes; taste for seasoning, and serve.

Vitello Ducale
Bertolucci's Restaurant, Pacific Grove

Yield: 4-6 servings

Note: Prepare Fish Stock and Fish Sauce in advance

Dino's Fish Stock

1 pound fillet of sole, or other white fish
prawn shells (empty, see Vitello Ducale recipe)
1 onion, cut into quarters
2 stalks celery, chopped
1 lemon, cut in half
3 bay leaves
4 ounces white wine
4 ounces cooking sherry
1 to 1 ½ gallons cold water

Bring all ingredients to a boil. Reduce heat and simmer for at least 4 hours, reducing stock to approximately 7 cups.

Fish Sauce

¾ cup butter
¾ cup flour
salt and pepper to taste
7 cups Dino's Fish Stock (above)

1. Melt butter and mix in flour to make roux. Add salt and pepper to taste.
2. Blend over low heat for at least 5 minutes, but do not brown.
3. Slowly pour in hot fish stock, stirring to blend and then cooking rapidly for 5 minutes until creamy.
4. Strain through a sieve to ensure that sauce is smooth.

Vitello Ducale

8 scallops or slices of veal, 3-4 ounces each
salt and pepper to taste
pinch finely chopped parsley
pinch finely chopped oregano
4 jumbo prawns, shelled, cleaned and butterflied,
**   with shells reserved**
1 cup flour
1 egg, beaten
Fish Sauce (above)
8 mushroom caps
1 ounce brandy or sherry
4 sprigs fresh parsley for garnish

Preheat oven to 375 degrees.
1. Lightly pound veal scallops and sprinkle each with salt, pepper, parsley and oregano.
2. Dip prepared prawns into flour, then into beaten egg and grill quickly on lightly oiled grill or in sauté pan until golden. Remove.
3. Place 1 grilled prawn on top of each of 4 slices of veal. Cover with remaining slices of veal and steady each serving with toothpicks on all 4 sides.
4. Dip each serving into flour, coating both sides, then quickly in and out of beaten egg. Grill on both sides until golden. Remove and set aside.
5. Line bottom of individual casseroles or 1 large baking dish with half of the fish sauce. Layer veal servings on top of sauce. Garnish with mushroom caps and top with remaining sauce.
6. Just before placing in oven, pour brandy or sherry over top. Bake in preheated oven for 15 to 20 minutes. Remove toothpicks before serving.
7. Garnish with sprigs of parsley and serve.

Linguine Pescadori
The Rogue, Monterey

Yield: 4 servings

8 scallops (20 to a pound)
8 prawns (15 to a pound), peeled
2 tablespoons olive oil
2 whole tomatoes, peeled, seeded and crushed
1 tablespoon fresh basil
1 tablespoon finely chopped garlic
4 sprigs fresh parsley, chopped
8 fresh clams
8 mussels
¼ cup water
16 ounces thin noodles (dry or fresh), cooked al dente
2 tablespoons sweet butter, unsalted
2 tablespoons heavy cream
1 tablespoon Parmesan cheese
salt to taste

1. Sauté scallops and prawns in 1 tablespoon of the olive oil in one pan.
2. In another pan, put the other tablespoon of oil and add tomatoes, basil, garlic and parsley.
3. Add clams and mussels to tomatoes; add ¼ cup water. Let simmer until they all open, then add scallops and prawns.
4. After noodles are cooked and drained, add sweet butter and heavy cream. Toss until hot and blended.
5. Put noodles on a platter. Remove seafood mixture with a slotted spoon and place on top of noodles.
6. Sprinkle cheese on top.

Monterey Bay Prawns

Sardine Factory, Monterey

Yield: 4-6 servings

**2 pounds medium sized Monterey Bay Prawns (large
    shrimp may be used)**
salt, pepper, paprika to taste
¹⁄₂ cup olive oil
15 cloves garlic, finely chopped
8 shallots, minced
1 cup white wine
¹⁄₂ cup white-wine vinegar
1 cup heavy cream
1 pound butter, cubed
salt and white pepper to taste
parsley

Preheat oven to 500 degrees.
1. Split prawns or shrimp, still in their shells, down the
   back. Sprinkle with salt, pepper and paprika.
2. Rub a baking sheet with enough of the olive oil to cover
   with a thin film, then rub with 1 teaspoon garlic.
3. Set prawns on baking sheet and bake at 500 degrees for
   4 minutes.
4. To prepare sauce, sauté shallots and rest of garlic in
   remaining olive oil. Add wine and vinegar and bring to a
   boil; continue boiling until the liquid is nearly evaporated.
5. Add cream and reduce by half to a thick consistency.
   Cut butter into cubes. If it gets too cold, you can heat
   the sauce slightly, but be careful not to boil it or it will
   liquefy. It should be just warm.
6. Season with salt and white pepper. Pour over prawns
   and sprinkle with parsley.

Monterey Bay Prawns with Butter and Chives

Club XIX, The Lodge at Pebble Beach

Yield: 4 servings

2 cups water
1 teaspoon salt
1 stalk celery with leaves, chopped
1 bay leaf
3 whole peppercorns
1 pound prawns, raw, in the shell
chive butter (see recipe)

Chive Butter (Make first)

½ cup softened butter
juice of ½ lemon
1 tablespoon chopped fresh chives
salt
freshly ground black pepper

1. In a small bowl, cream the butter, lemon juice and chives with a wooden spoon until soft and fluffy.
2. Season with salt and pepper.

Prawns

1. Bring water to a rolling boil in a large pot.
2. Add the salt, celery, bay leaf and peppercorns and boil for 2 minutes.
3. Drop in the prawns. As soon as the water returns to a full boil, remove from heat.
4. Drain, shell and devein prawns while still warm. Keep them warm on a platter. Top with chive butter. Serve with snow peas and tomatoes.

Scampi

The Rogue, Monterey

Yield: 1 serving

7-8 prawns (15 to a pound)
flour for dredging
2 ounces butter, clarified
2 ounces water
½ teaspoon chopped, fresh garlic
½ lemon
1 tablespoon chopped parsley
2 tablespoons sweet butter, unsalted

1. Remove shells from prawns; leave tail.
2. Dredge in flour; sauté in clarified butter over hot flame.
3. Add water, garlic, lemon and parsley. Take off fire and add sweet butter.
4. Shake pan to incorporate butter to make sauce.

Cranberry-Stuffed Game Hens

The Tap Room, The Lodge at Pebble Beach

Yield: 4 servings

3 cups breadcrumbs
salt
white pepper
³/₄ teaspoon each chopped fresh thyme, marjoram, rosemary and sage
4 game hens
salt and pepper
¹/₄ pound bacon, chopped
1 medium onion, chopped
¹/₄ cup chopped celery
¹/₂ cup cranberries, fresh or frozen
¹/₃ cup chopped pecans
1 6-ounce can frozen orange juice concentrate, thawed
¹/₂ cup water
1 teaspoon aromatic bitters

1. To prepare the stuffing, toast the breadcrumbs in a 300-degree oven for 30 minutes, or until hard and brown. In a small bowl, toss the crumbs with ¹/₄ teaspoon salt, pepper and herbs. Set aside.
2. Preheat the oven to 400 degrees. Wash the hens under cold water and pat dry. Sprinkle the birds inside and out with salt and pepper.
3. In a heavy skillet, over medium heat, fry the bacon until crisp. Remove and drain on paper towel. Lower the heat to medium and sauté the onion and celery in the bacon fat for 5 minutes.
4. Remove the skillet from the heat and stir in the cranberries, nuts and breadcrumb mixture.
5. In a small bowl, mix the orange juice, water and bitters. Pour ¹/₂ of this mixture into the cranberry stuffing and reserve the rest for basting the birds.
6. Stir the stuffing until it is well blended and all the liquid is absorbed. Fill each bird, sew or skewer the opening and tie the legs together.

7. Put the stuffed birds on the rack of a shallow roasting pan. Roast in the middle of the oven for 1 hour or until the birds are tender, basting with orange juice mixture every 15 minutes.
8. Remove the birds to a warm platter and serve with the pan juices spooned over them.

Poulet de Broccoli

The Steinbeck House, Salinas

Yield: 8 servings

2 ²/₃ cups cooked chicken, breast and thigh
2 10-ounce packages frozen broccoli, or fresh broccoli

1. Barely cook broccoli spears. (Slash stems for more even cooking.)
2. Put in a buttered casserole or ramekin. Add a layer of chicken which has been torn into chunky pieces.

Sauce

2 10-ounce cans cream of chicken soup
1 cup mayonnaise
1 teaspoon lemon juice
¹/₂ teaspoon curry powder

Mix above ingredients together and cover the chicken and broccoli.

Topping

1 ¹/₄ cups sharp Cheddar cheese, shredded
1 ¹/₄ cups soft bread cubes mixed with 2 tablespoons melted butter

Preheat oven to 350 degrees.
1. Cover sauce with the cheese.
2. Top with the bread mixture.
3. Bake at 350 degrees for 30 minutes.

Chocolate Mousse

Hog's Breath Inn, Carmel-by-the-Sea

Yield: 5 servings

¾ **pound chocolate**
4 eggs
2 cups powdered sugar
½ **pint whipping cream**
2 ounces plain brandy

1. Melt chocolate.
2. Separate eggs.
3. Whip egg whites until fluffy, meringue style.
4. Combine egg whites, sugar, and whipping cream. Whip until heavy, about 3-4 minutes.
5. Combine egg yolks and brandy and add to egg-white mixture; blend on slow speed for 3-4 minutes. Add chocolate and blend until mixed well.
6. Pour into dessert glasses; chill for 1 hour or until firm.

Trifle

The Covey at Quail Lodge, Carmel Valley

Yield: 12 servings

5 whole eggs
5 egg yolks
1½ to 2 cups sugar
4 cups whipped cream
6 ounces shredded chocolate
1 ounce gelatin
6 ounces dry sherry or cognac
1 dozen macaroon almond cookies

1. Whip whole eggs and yolks with sugar until light and fluffy.
2. Fold in whipped cream and chocolate.
3. Melt gelatin in sherry; cool and fold into whipped cream mixture.
4. Pour pudding into 12 wine glasses and lay the macaroons in the middle of pudding.
5. Keep in refrigerator for a few hours before serving.

Fresh Fruit Daiquiri
The Lodge at Pebble Beach

(See photograph)

Yield: 1 serving

1 ½ ounces fresh lemon juice
2 teaspoons sugar
3 tablespoons raspberries or other fruit
1 ½ ounces light rum

Blend above ingredients with crushed ice. Serve with sprig of fresh mint.

Del Monte Fizz
The Lodge at Pebble Beach

Yield: 1 serving

1 ounce fresh orange juice
1 ounce fresh lemon juice
1 ¼ ounces gin
2 ounces half & half
1 egg white
1 teaspoon vanilla extract
1-2 teaspoons sugar

1. Sweeten to taste with 1 or 2 teaspoons sugar.
2. Blend with ice.

Additional Information

Weights and Measures

3 teaspoons	1 tablespoon
2 tablespoons	1 liquid ounce
4 tablespoons	¼ cup
16 tablespoons	1 cup
2 wine glasses	¼ cup
2 cups	1 pint
2 pints	1 quart
4 quarts	1 gallon
8 quarts	1 peck
4 pecks	1 bushel
16 ounces	1 pound
3 medium apples	1 pound
½ cup butter	¼ pound
2 cups butter	1 pound
2 tablespoons butter	1 ounce
2 cups cottage cheese	1 pound
2 cups cream cheese	1 pound
4 cups grated hard cheese	1 pound
1 square chocolate	1 ounce
1 ounce chocolate	⅓ cup cocoa
5 cups shredded coconut	1 pound

Flour, sifted

4 cups all-purpose	1 pound
4½ cups cake	1 pound
3½ cups whole wheat	1 pound
4½ to 5 cups rye	1 pound
1 lemon, juice	2½ to 3½ teaspoons
4 cups macaroni 1-inch pieces	1 pound

6 cups noodles 1-inch pieces . . . . . . .1 pound
1 orange, juice. . . . . .5 to 6 teaspoons
3 medium onions . . . . .1 pound
2 cups dried peas or beans . . . . .1 pound
3 medium potatoes . . . . .1 pound
2 cups rice. .1 pound
Sugar
    2 cups granulated . . . . .1 pound
    2¼ cups packed brown . . . . .1 pound
    3½ cups sifted confectioners . . . .1 pound
3 medium tomatoes . . . . .1 pound
8 ounce can. . . . . .1 cup
No. 1 can. . . . . .2 cups
No. 2 can. . . . . .2 cups
No. 2½ can .3 cups
No. 3 can. . . . . .4 cups
No. 10 can. .13 cups

Metric Conversion Tables

Liquid Measure:
    1 teaspoon   = 5 cubic centimeters
    1 tablespoon = 15 cubic centimeters
    1 ounce   = 30 milliliters
    1 cup   = about ¼ liter
    1 quart   = about 1 liter
To determine liquid measure multiply

The number of:	By	To Get
ounces	30	milliliters
pints	0.47	liters
quarts	0.95	liters

Dry Measure:
    1 ounce = about 28 grams
    1 pound = about 454 grams
To determine dry measure multiply

The number of:	By	To Get
ounces	28	grams
pounds	0.45	grams

Food Measurements:
Sugar:
    1 tablespoon = 15 grams
    1 cup   = 240 grams

Salt:
    1 tablespoon = 15 grams
Flour:
    ¼ cup   = 35 grams
    1 cup   = 140 grams
Rice:
    1 cup   = 240 grams
Butter:
    1 tablespoon = 15 grams
    ½ cup   = 125 grams

Celebrity Golfers Index

Alcott, Amy
Marinated Chicken
Véronique, 154
My Favorite Chocolate Bar,
244
Pomegranate Lamb, 117
Rice and Artichoke Salad, 54
Berg, Patty
Easy Meatloaf, 108
Boone, The Pat Boone Family
Chili à la Boone, 97
Booth, Dana
Dana's Refrigerator
Cheesecake, 208
Brannan, Michael
Cheese and Bacon Spread,
13
Bryant, Brad
Enchiladas Texas Style, 102
Fruit Salad with Dressing, 51
Burke, Jim
French Onion Soup, 38
Burns III, George
Favorite Chicken Salad, 49
Italian Stuffed Meatloaf, 109
Campbell, Glen
Chili con Carne, 98
Casper, Billy
Billy's Scrumptious Cream
Pie, 218
Coles, Janet
Carmel Omelette, 74
Coody, Charles
Chili Relleno Dip, 15
Cook, John
Cook's Chili, 99
Conner, Frank
Ritzy Cracker Pie, 230

Coward, Mark
Baked Beans, 170
Creamed Jalapeño Shrimp in
Patty Shells, 139
19th Hole Frozen Margaritas,
258
Spidery Haystack Cookies,
244
Sweet and Sour Asparagus,
169
Clampett, Bobby
Chicken Fantastic, 150
Crafter, Jane
Jane's Vienna Schnitzel,
Aussie Style, 122
Crenshaw, Ben D.
Cheesecake Bars, 238
Crosby, Kathryn
After Golf Cookies, 237
Cupit, Jacky
Green Enchilada Casserole,
103
De Armar, Marlene Floyd
Chuck Roast, 101
Diehl, Terry
Apple Salad with Honey
Peanut Dressing, 46
Dodge, Sally
Sweet Chocolate Cake, 210
Doss, Jack
Green Chili Cheese Dip, 16
Pepperidge Farm Chicken
Breasts, 157
Eastwood, Bob
Marinated Flank Steak, 104
Eastwood, Clint
Hole-In-One Chicken, 152
Fiori, Ed
South Texas Fried Bass, 125
Fleckman, Marty
Shrimp Casserole, 137
Fleisher, Bruce
Hot Artichoke Cheese Dip, 7
Floyd, Ray
Raymond's Spicy Chili, 100

Index

The authors have attempted to obtain original recipes from the many
contributors to this volume. If copyright material has inadvertently been
included, the authors and publisher would appreciate being advised so that
complete credit can be included in future editions of this book.